DISCIPLES
— OF ALL —
NATIONS

CONTINUOUS MISSION UNTIL HE COMES

JOHN L. AMSTUTZ

STUDY GUIDE BY GARY MATSDORF

DISCIPLES OF ALL NATIONS
CONTINUOUS MISSION UNTIL HE COMES

Published by Foursquare Missions International/Foursquare Media
1910 W. Sunset Blvd.
Los Angeles, CA 90026
www.foursquaremedia.org

All Scripture quotations are taken from the Holy Bible, New International Version®, NIV®. Copyright © 1973, 1978, 1984 by International Bible Society. Used by permission of Zondervan Publishing House.

ISBN 978-0-9802392-4-9
Printed in the United States of America

Contents

Disciples of All Nations:
Continuous Mission Until He Comes

The weight of a book is determined by neither the scales at the post office nor the renown of its author. Its true weight is determined by the imprint it leaves on lives—through content that begets timeless and transforming results. By that measure, this book weighs a ton! And I'm pleased to be asked to invite you into its pages—a foreword intended to prompt you forward.

John L. Amstutz, the author, has characterized the heart of that "call" that leaders in the living Church have always been intended to address: "Go and make disciples of all nations" (Matthew 28:19). He has given us these pages as a reflection of what has characterized his own life mission for the thirty-five years I have known him. John is serious about Jesus' call to "make disciples." It's the only way I have ever known him to be, and it has been the focus of his entire ministry.

Through this handbook, John has framed a resource to enable Christian leaders to grasp and apply the elements of effective discipleship and the multiplication of disciples and, thereby, churches. His work directs us to Jesus' plan for making disciples, and also helps us sense the Holy Spirit's passion for relentless advance of the Gospel until the Savior's return. This handbook is a tool to serve the whole Body of Christ—a fundamental priority of our movement, which is dedicated to "worldwide and interdenominational evangelism."

Two primary values compel both the Foursquare movement and our release of this publication:

1. We want to focus the purpose and the power Jesus gives believers when the Holy Spirit "comes upon" them—targeting global witness to His saving life and power.
2. We want to fulfill that mission in partnership with all who bear Jesus' Name—teaming with His servants throughout the whole Church to reach and teach (disciple) then plant and establish local churches (evangelize)—always, everywhere, and beyond sectarian smallness.

As you enter these pages, I invite you to experience the promise of God's Kingdom grace and power in the face of profound need in our world. The whole Church is being called back from superficial notions that "church growth" is what Jesus planned, when in fact it was (and is) "people growth" that advances His Church as His disciples sink their roots in His Word, on the banks of the Holy Spirit's stream of nourishing resource through His presence and gifts.

Rooted in those realities, which define how the Church was conceived and how it will multiply life to the nations, we open to Christ's timeless promise and potential for our dynamic enablement and durable fruitfulness—unto "continuous mission until He comes"—as His disciples, and as His disciple-makers.

Jack W. Hayford
President, Foursquare Church International
Founding Pastor, The Church On The Way

Acknowledgements

The contributions of many made this manual possible. Don McGregor, missionary, strategist, teacher, and friend has been an exemplary practitioner who has both modeled and mentored a generation of Foursquare missionaries in the making of disciples of the nations. Frank Greer, Ted Olbrich, Lee Schnabel, and Mark Shaw are among numerous missionaries who have been instrumental in developing national church movements. Their stories from the field represent the many more that could be told, including those of Wilson Badejo, Leslie Keegel, and Josue Bengston, national leaders who have led their countries in discipling nations. The teaching and writing of field missionaries Greg Fisher, Bill Kieselhorst, Glen Mickel, and the late John Louwerse contributed significantly to understanding, communicating, and implementing the developmental process in many countries.

Special words of thanks go to Johnell Loop, who patiently oversaw the development of this manual; to Gary Matsdorf, who wrote the accompanying study guide; to Wanda Brackett, who edited the entire manuscript; to Mark Mickel, who created the cover design; to Michelle Glush who formatted the text; and to Rick Wulfestieg, who facilitated and expedited publication.

The encouragement of Jonathan Hall, the director of Foursquare Missions International, and that of his predecessor, Mike Larkin, greatly aided the release and distribution of this manual. The foreword by Pastor Jack W. Hayford, president of The Foursquare Church, certainly does "prompt us forward" in making disciples of all nations; it clearly expresses the heart of our Savior, Jesus Christ, to whose glory this work is dedicated.

Preface

The gospel is expanding. The number of believers is increasing. Followers of Jesus Christ are multiplying. Today the Church is growing. Jesus is building His Church. Since the death and resurrection of Jesus Christ 2000 years ago, there have been periods of expansion and retreat of the Christian faith. Although there has been decline during the past century in the western world, the gospel has expanded rapidly in Latin America, Africa and Asia from less than 100 million in 1900 to more than one billion in 2000. As a result the Church has become, for the first time since the Day of Pentecost, truly global. Followers of Jesus Christ are now found in every inhabited country on earth.[1]

Such rapid growth and globalization has characterized an increasing number of Christian movements, especially the Pentecostal and Charismatic movements.[2] This includes the Foursquare movement. From less than 3,500 churches and meeting places in 32 countries in 1975, The Foursquare Church has grown to more than 50,000 churches and meeting places in nearly 140 countries.[3]

From its beginning in the 1920s the Foursquare movement has been "dedicated unto to the cause of inter-denominational and world wide evangelism."[4] The command of Jesus Christ to "make disciples of all nations" is the foundation of the International Church of the Foursquare Gospel. To fulfill its biblical purpose and historic mission, The Foursquare Church has sought to follow the pattern of Spirit-empowered church development found in the New Testament by evangelizing, releasing indigenous leadership, cultivating church planting and reproducing missionary-sending churches. In other words, the Foursquare movement is committed to the development of strong, reproducing national churches. Both the history of the first-century Church and the history of the Foursquare movement have confirmed the need for developing infinitely reproducible churches that make possible the continuous spread of the gospel to those yet unreached. Therefore, the pattern of a four-stage developmental process has been intentionally taught and increasingly practiced by national churches around the world.

Clearly the Lord has blessed the advance of the gospel through the global Foursquare Church. The shift in missions focus toward and the increasing involvement of the local church is an encouraging and significant trend. This, along with the rapid growth and globalization of The Foursquare Church, underscores the need for clarifying and communicating our "Foursquare missiology," how and why we do missions. For teaching and training of pastors, missions leaders, missionaries and national leaders this book is written, to the glory of God and the advance of His kingdom...until He comes.

John L. Amstutz
April 2008

Disciples of All Nations:
Luke's Story

"Then Jesus came to them and said,
'All authority in heaven and on earth has been given to me.
Therefore go and make disciples of all nations.'"
(Matthew 28:18, 19)

"Disciples of *all* nations"—amazing! Did Jesus really expect eleven working class Galilean Jews to reach an *entire* world with the gospel? Apparently he did, for he told them the gospel of the kingdom would be preached "in the *whole* world as a testimony to *all* nations" (Matthew 24:14). If Jesus had this in mind, he must have made adequate preparation for it to happen. He did! He promised his authority, his presence and his power. And what did his disciples do with what they were given by the risen Christ? They preached the gospel and planted churches wherever they went.

The expansion of the gospel in the first century was remarkable. Less than a decade after Pentecost, Luke could write, "The church throughout Judea, Galilee and Samaria...was strengthened, and encouraged by the Holy Spirit, it grew in numbers, living in the fear of the Lord" (Acts 9:31). Less than three decades after Pentecost, the Apostle Paul wrote, "From Jerusalem all the way around to Illyricum (Albania), I have fully proclaimed the gospel of Christ...Now there is no more place for me to work in these regions" (Romans 15:19, 23). And shortly thereafter, Paul penned these amazing words to the Colossian church: "All over the (Roman) world this gospel is producing fruit and growing...This is the gospel that you heard and that has been proclaimed to every creature under heaven, and of which I, Paul, have become a servant" (Colossians 1:6, 23). "Disciples of all nations" was well on its way as the gospel was proclaimed and churches were planted throughout the Roman Empire.[1] Let's look at the Book of Acts and see if we can discover how the Early Church developed into a movement that penetrated the entire Roman Empire.

Luke, a Gentile doctor, tells the story. It all began with Pentecost—the foundation of all expansion Jesus had promised that it would be "after the Holy Spirit comes on you" that "you will be my witnesses in Jerusalem, in all Judea and Samaria, and to the ends of the earth" (Acts 1:8). And so it was. When the Spirit came on the 120 in the upper room, they began speaking in other languages. Fifteen different nations are mentioned who heard the Galileans speaking "in their own native language" the "wonderful works of God" (Acts 2:7-12). Babel's confusion of tongues was being reversed. And of these 3,000 responded to Peter's message and believed, were baptized, and received the promise of the Father, the Holy Spirit, given to all whom the Lord God calls (Acts 2:38-40). The "making of disciples of the *nations*" had begun...in Jerusalem.

Luke's fascinating story in the Book of Acts relates this expanding witness of first-century disciples "in Jerusalem, and in all Judea and Samaria, and to the ends of the earth" (Acts 1:8). A closer look reveals a "tale of key cities," namely, cities such as Jerusalem in Palestine, Antioch in Syria, and Ephesus in western Turkey. In each case a church planting movement developed that both penetrated the surrounding area and launched the witness of the gospel into new regions as the gospel spread among the nations beginning with the Jews.

A National Movement among the Jews

Luke's vivid account begins with the witness of the twelve apostles in **Jerusalem in Palestine** on the Day of Pentecost. Three thousand repented and were baptized (Acts 2:37-41). In subsequent weeks and months, those new believers became disciples of Jesus Christ, devoting themselves to "the apostles' teaching, to the fellowship, to the breaking of bread and to prayer. Everyone was filled with awe, and many wonders and miraculous signs were done by the apostles" (Acts 2:42, 43). What was the result? "The Lord added to their number daily those who were being saved" until "the number of the men (alone!) grew to about 5,000" (Acts 2:47; 4:4). Even after the untimely deaths of Ananias and Sapphira, the Church continued to grow and increase so that "more and more men and women believed in the Lord and were added to their number" (Acts 5:14).

Opposition from jealous Jewish religious leaders resulted in threats against and imprisonment of the disciples. But this only emboldened their witness. "They never stopped teaching and proclaiming the good news that Jesus is the messiah" (Acts 5:42). In fact, the increase of believers caused a problem not only for their antagonists but also for the Church. Foreign born Hellenistic (Greek-speaking) Jews complained the native born Hebrew (Aramaic-speaking) Jews were overlooking their widows in the daily distribution of food. What could have caused division was dealt with wisely. Unity was preserved, and the leadership base was expanded to include seven Hellenistic Jewish men who were chosen by the Church and set apart by the twelve Aramaic-speaking apostles to oversee the daily distribution (Acts 6:1-6). And so "the word of God spread. The number of disciples in Jerusalem increased rapidly, and a large number of priests became obedient to the faith" (Acts 6:7). Within a short time the Church was found throughout Judea and Galilee (Acts 9:31). A national movement was in the making among the Jews. "Disciples of all nations" was taking place first within the Jewish nation through the multiplication of churches throughout Palestine.

A National Movement among the Samaritans

Then it happened—martyrdom. Stephen, one of "the seven," was put to death for his witness. Driven out of Jerusalem by the persecution, Hellenists Jews such as Philip took the gospel to Samaria where there was "great joy in that city" as many believed and were baptized (Acts 8:8). News of this reached Jerusalem, and Peter and John were sent to confirm the validity of the conversion of the Samaritans. Confirmation came quickly, for, as they laid hands on the new believers, they too received the Holy Spirit. Peter and John then preached the gospel "in many Samaritan villages" (Acts 8:25), and the gospel began to spread throughout the Samaritan nation. The result was a church "throughout Samaria" as well as throughout Judea and Galilee. Furthermore, one of the chief persecutors, Saul of Tarsus, was converted to Christ and would become an apostle to the Gentiles (non-Jewish nations). Even Peter himself, in obedience to a heavenly vision, found himself preaching the gospel in the home of Cornelius, a Gentile God-fearer whose entire household believed, was filled with the Holy Spirit, and baptized (Acts 10). Amazed, the leaders of the Jerusalem church praised God declaring, "God has even granted the Gentiles repentance unto life" (Acts 11:18).

National Movements among the Gentiles

Meanwhile, others "who had been scattered by the persecution in connection with Stephen traveled as far as Phoenicia (Lebanon), Cyprus, and Antioch (Syria) telling the message only to Jews" (Acts 11:19). However, some men from Cyrene (North Africa) and Cyprus "went to Antioch and began to speak to Greeks also" and "a great number of people believed and turned to the Lord" (Acts 11:20, 21). And so the Jewish church, involuntarily forced out of Jerusalem because of persecution, moved into non-Jewish territory with the gospel both within and beyond Palestine. **Antioch in Syria** became a key center in the expansion of the gospel.

As had occurred in Jerusalem, the believers in Antioch also were instructed in the way of the Lord. "For a whole year Barnabas and Saul [Paul] met with the church and taught great numbers of people" (Acts 11:25,26a). Not only did Jews believe, but many Gentiles turned to the Lord at Antioch where "the disciples were first called Christians" (Acts 11:26b). The composite Greek and Latin word "Christian" was now used to describe a composite people made up of both Jews and Greeks. Again, as had occurred in Jerusalem, the church's growth required additional leaders. In this case, three "foreigners" joined Barnabas and Paul in leadership, "Simeon called Niger, Lucius of Cyrene and Manaen (who had been brought up with Herod the tetrarch)" (Acts 13:1). This time expansion of the gospel came voluntarily. In obedience to the word of the Spirit, Barnabas and Paul were set apart for the work to which they had been called. With fasting and prayer the church at Antioch sent them off to Cyprus and Turkey. When they returned about two years later, they "gathered the church together and reported "all that God had done through them and how He had opened the door of faith to the Gentiles" (Acts 14:27). A church planting movement had begun among the Gentiles. "Disciples of all nations" now included Gentile nations. Such evangelism among non-Jews caused some Jewish believers in Jerusalem to call into question the validity of the conversion of uncircumcised Gentiles. The apostles and elders at Jerusalem, after much debate with Barnabas and Paul, concluded that they "should not make it difficult for the Gentiles who are turning to God" (Acts 15:19). They agreed with Peter's testimony concerning Cornelius' household: "God, who knows the heart, showed that He accepted them (Gentiles) by giving the Holy Spirit to them, just as He did to us (Jews). He made no distinction between us and them, for He purified their hearts by faith" (Acts 15:8, 9). Therefore, Gentiles should not be circumcised. "No! We believe it is through the grace of our Lord Jesus that we are saved" (Acts 15:11). In other words, Gentiles were not required to become Jews to be Christians. They were simply instructed to observe several prohibitions found in the Law of Moses lest Jewish believers would be offended (Acts 15:19-21). These requirements had nothing to do with salvation. Apparently they were intended to encourage right relationships between Gentiles and Jews. When this decision was reported to the Gentile churches, "they were glad for its encouraging message" (Acts 15:31).

The result of the Jerusalem Council's wise decision was the full release of Gentile evangelism. Such evangelism was illustrated most dramatically through the Apostle Paul. From the time of his Damascus Road conversion, Paul knew he was called to be an apostle to the Gentiles, for he had "received grace and apostleship to call people from among all the Gentiles to the obedience that comes from faith" (Romans 1:5). And so, the church at Antioch sent him, Silas and Timothy on another mission to the Gentiles. In addition to the churches pioneered on the first journey in south central Turkey, new churches were started in Greece as Paul answered the "Macedonian vision" and took the gospel to Europe (Acts 16).

Perhaps one of the most powerful penetrations of a region took place on Paul's third journey when he spent three years in **Ephesus in western Turkey**. It began with twelve disciples of John the Baptist who were "baptized into the name of the Lord Jesus" and filled with the Spirit (Acts 19:5, 6). Although many Jews refused to believe, Paul found the Gentiles open. For two years he had daily discussions about the gospel in the hall of Tyrannus, and the Lord did "extraordinary miracles" through Paul. Meanwhile, the apostle also taught the whole counsel of God, both publicly and from house to house, making disciples of those who believed. Thus the church grew and was strengthened. It was purified from idol worship and magical practices. "In this way the word of the Lord spread widely and grew in power" (Acts 19:20). Ephesus, formerly noted for its idol worship, became a center for the spread of the gospel. Discipled converts, such as Epaphras from Colosse, returned to their hometowns to share the good news of Jesus Christ (Colossians 1:7). As a result churches were planted in Colosse, Hierapolis, Laodicea and throughout the Lycus Valley. A province-wide church planting movement was born in western Turkey. As a result "all the Jews and Greeks who lived in the province of Asia heard the word of the Lord" (Acts 19:10).

Lest we misunderstand, this rapid expansion of the gospel was wider than the ministry of just the apostles. For example, Luke makes it clear that the church in Rome was there long before Paul arrived. The "making of disciples of all nations" was carried out by a Spirit-filled and Spirit-directed Church that, along with the apostles, became a witness to the ends of the earth. And although this expansion of the gospel was spontaneous, it was not without design. Luke's account in Acts makes clear that the "making of disciples of all nations" happened because the gospel took root and bore fruit through the establishing of healthy, mature, culturally appropriate, reproducing churches in key centers such as Jerusalem, Antioch, and Ephesus. Through such churches the gospel "branched out" into movements that penetrated surrounding regions.[2] Eventually, either intentionally or unintentionally, believers also took the gospel into the "regions beyond." And so, from Jerusalem through Judea and Samaria, the gospel headed for "the ends of the earth" as believers took the good news of Jesus Christ to the entire Mediterranean world. They evangelized in-depth through the teaching of new believers. They evangelized widely through the planting of new churches. This was their ongoing response to their risen Lord's commission to "make disciples of all nations." For this His promised power, presence, and authority were given.

A Biblical Pattern of National Church Development

What patterns are evident in Luke's fascinating story? We can see at least four essential phases or stages in the development of these earliest "national church movements" which penetrated regions, cultural groups, and, eventually, the entire Roman Empire.[3] These four stages were involved in the development of national movements among people with common culture and language:

A. An Initiating Stage: preaching the gospel and planting the church in a key center (*Acts 2:42-47*)

B. A Nurturing Stage: strengthening the church and developing leaders (*Acts 6:1-7*)

C. An Expanding Stage: structuring the church and multiplying churches throughout a region (*Acts 8:25; 9:31*)

D. A Sending Stage: extending the church and sending missionaries (*Acts 11:26-19; 13:1-3*)

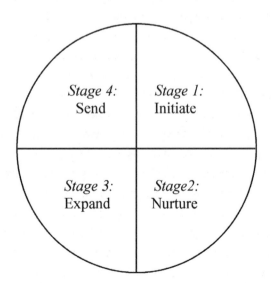

In key religious, political, and cultural centers such as Jerusalem, Antioch, and Ephesus there was an *initiating stage*, in which the gospel was preached in the power of the Holy Spirit and a church was started. Those who repented and believed the gospel were baptized, filled with the Spirit, incorporated into the fellowship of believers, and taught what Christ had commanded. The result was disciples who began to multiply themselves as they shared the good news about Jesus Christ with family and friends.

A *nurturing stage* followed as these new disciples received both teaching and modeling in "sound doctrine," that is, the practical application of faith in Christ in the home and the community. As the number of disciples increased, those who learned to lead their homes well became leaders in the emerging church. The growing number of maturing and gifted leaders both strengthened the church and made possible the multiplication of additional fellowships.

An *expanding stage* began to take shape as a church took root in the culture and began to structure and express itself in a way that fit the situation, and it became self-supporting, self-governing, and self-propagating. The multiplication of leaders led to the multiplication of new churches. The result was an emerging national church movement that eventually penetrated an entire region and culture.

An important *sending stage* took place when the national church began to take the gospel to other cultures and peoples, as believers reached out to those who had not yet heard or understood the gospel. So the developmental process was repeated within a new group as the gospel was preached and new churches started, making possible the continuous spread of the gospel to all cultures and groups.

Conclusion

From Luke's story in Acts, these, then, are the basic stages that help us understand how the Early Church developed into an empire-penetrating movement as it sought to carry out its Master's mandate to "make disciples of all nations." The Church in the Book of Acts reproduced that which was "infinitely repro-ducible," namely, *obedient disciples, godly leaders, new congregations and national missionary-sending church movements.* This "infinitely reproducible life cycle" is how the Early Church sought to fulfill Christ's last command to reach the world by making "disciples of all *nations.*" It can be done! They did it. It must be done! "For this gospel of the kingdom shall be preached in all the world as a witness to every *nation*" before the end comes (Matthew 24:14). "Disciples of every nation" requires national church movements in every *nation.* It can be done! It must be done!

CHAPTER ONE

Disciples of All Nations:
Foursquare's Story

"**D**edicated unto the cause of inter-denominational and world wide evangelism"—these words, inscribed on the primary cornerstone of Angelus Temple, express the purpose, spirit, and scope of the Foursquare movement. From its inception in the 1920s, The Foursquare Church has been dedicated to world evangelization, seeking to be interdenominational in spirit and international in scope. In the words of its founder, Aimee Semple McPherson, the International Church of the Foursquare Gospel was called to "unity in essentials, liberty in non-essentials, and charity in all things." Its assignment was to go "around the world with the Foursquare gospel" of Jesus Christ who is "the Savior, the Healer, the Baptizer with the Holy Spirit, and the coming King."[1]

Sister McPherson believed the Foursquare movement was to play a part in restoring that which was lost.[2] Because "Jesus Christ is the same yesterday, today and forever" (Hebrews 13:8), the life, vitality, and growth of the first-century church was also available in the twentieth century by the power of the Holy Spirit. Pentecost was more than an event. It was an experience, making available the Spirit's power to every believer in every generation. And as such, it released the power for worldwide witness today as it did in the first century. Angelus Temple and the Foursquare movement it birthed became an example of the vitality and validity of New Testament church life and growth in the twentieth century.

Latin America

No wonder many of the early Foursquare pioneer missionaries, baptized in the Holy Spirit, sought either intuitively or intentionally to follow the example of the Church in the Book of Acts.[3] They saw what was happening in North America. Why should it not happen abroad? And it did—first in **Latin America**. Typical is what took place through the Arthur Edwards family that went to Panama in 1928. In those days missionary work was focused primarily on tribal people in rural parts. Since Panama was largely untouched with the gospel, Rev. Edwards felt he should follow the Apostle Paul's example.[4] Although a fruitful work took place in Frijoles in the center of the country, he believed that strong churches in major population centers would be the key to reaching the rural areas. So the Edwardses began work in cities, starting with the capital, Panama City. Both Rev. and Mrs. Edwards preached, and the Lord confirmed the message with signs following. Healing, in particular, opened many doors for the gospel as many came to Christ. New converts were discipled and nurtured, and the church began to grow. Within several years a strong Foursquare youth movement led by their son, Leland Edwards, produced many dedicated young people who regularly met for worship, Bible study, and evangelism. A Bible training school was started, and students regularly went to villages to evangelize. Additional Foursquare missionaries were sent and churches were opened in several provincial capitals. A national movement began to develop, and by 1940 The Foursquare Church was the largest protestant movement in Panama, with 60 churches. In 1950 Foursquare missionaries Rev. and Mrs. Vinton Johnson began evangelizing among the Choco Indians in the remote jungles of the Darien Province. Today there are more than 600 churches scattered throughout the country of Panama, representing more than 50,000 believers.

The Foursquare Church in Panama also began ministry in Colombia. In 1930, Harmodio Palacio, a Panamanian converted under the ministry of Arthur and Edith Edwards, returned to his hometown in Colombia and led his entire family to the Lord. Several churches were started in villages along the Atrato River. Later Palacio returned to Panama to work in the Darien Province and was unable, because of distance, to care for the churches. Thus, another evangelical mission took over those congregations. However, in 1943 two experienced missionary families who had served in the jungles of Bolivia for more than ten years were sent to Colombia. Instead of continuing to focus exclusively on rural areas, they, as the Edwardses had done, wisely chose to begin in a city. They chose Bucaramanga, the largest city in the province, which had a population of 50,000. Although intense religious opposition persisted for more than fifteen years throughout Colombia, the Foursquare work began to grow steadily. Even persecution and death could not prevent the spread of the gospel. Instead of fighting their persecutors, the missionaries faithfully taught the Word and trained a growing number of young people, many who later became national leaders in the Colombian Foursquare Church. From Bucaramunga the Foursquare work spread to cities such as Barranquilla and Cartagena on the north coast and Bogota, the capital, in the center of the country. Today more than 100,000 Colombians are found meeting regularly in over 800 Foursquare churches and meeting places throughout the nation. Colombian workers have also pioneered churches in the neighboring countries of Venezuela and Peru.

A strong pioneering spirit focused on population centers has produced similar national church movements throughout Central and South America. Foursquare missionaries from North America and nationals from neighboring Latin countries initiated church planting movements in Mexico (1943), Brazil (1946), Chile (1947), Honduras (1952), Costa Rica (1952),

Nicaragua (1952), Guatemala (1955), Venezuela (1955), Argentina (1955), Ecuador (1956), El Salvador (1973), Uruguay (1980), and Paraguay (1986). The result initially made Foursquare somewhat of a Latin American movement. Today more than one-third of all Foursquare churches are still found in Central and South America, with Brazil accounting for two-thirds of these Latin churches.

Africa

Meanwhile, national church movements also began to develop in **Africa**. Although Foursquare work began as early as 1928 in the Congo/Zaire and 1929 in South Africa, it was not until 1954 that a strong national movement took place in Sub-Saharan Africa.[5] Rev. and Mrs. Harold Curtis began the Foursquare work in the Yaba area of the capital city of Lagos, holding evangelistic street meetings and conducting a Sunday school. Among those saved were J. A. Boyejo and Samuel Odunaika who later became leaders of the national church. A Bible institute was begun with forty night school students and seventy correspondence students. In 1956 T. L. Osborn conducted an evangelistic crusade in Lagos and had up to 45,000 in attendance. Many were saved and healed, and hundreds of converts became part of The Foursquare Church. Miss Audra Sowersby, the traveling tutor of the Osborn's children, remained in Nigeria to assist the Curtises in the Bible institute, for the number of students was increasing rapidly. As a result churches began to multiply, pioneered and led by those dedicated students. Other American missionaries were sent to assist in the development of the growing church. The outbreak of the tragic civil was in Biafra in eastern Nigeria in 1967 had two important effects on The Foursquare Church. The Foursquare work, largely carried out among the Yoruba tribe in the southwest, began to expand into the Ibo tribe in the east where the war had taken place. As a result the church was working among a second major tribe. "Home missions" was happening. Second, the civil war strained relationships between nationals and foreign missionaries. Thus, serious steps were taken to nationalize the work. In 1971 Rev. Samuel Odunaika was appointed national supervisor and chairman of the national board. The missionaries became advisors and trainers, and the work grew even more rapidly. By 1981 there were 99 churches, and 10 had more than 1,000 attending Sunday services each week. Today there are more than 3,000 churches and meeting places, with more than 200,000 attending each Sunday. Furthermore, the Nigerian church sent and supported missionaries who opened Foursquare works in Benin (1970), Ghana (1974), Liberia (1981), Kenya (1984), Sierra Leone (1989), and the Central African Republic (1991). In turn the Kenya Foursquare Church sent a missionary to pioneer Tanzania (1989), which resulted in the pioneering of Foursquare works in Burundi and Rwanda in 1989.

Today there are Foursquare churches found in more than thirty Sub-Saharan countries, and it is The Foursquare Church in Nigeria that has directly or indirectly been responsible for pioneering many of those countries. Although most of the Foursquare works in the countries of Sub-Saharan Africa are young, as the church in Latin America, they are seeking to follow the Book of Acts by preaching the gospel and planting churches in urban areas. The goal is to penetrate their country and cultures with a national church planting movement, much like what is happening in Nigeria.

Asia

In **Asia** a similar pattern has developed. The oldest Foursquare work is in the Philippines, pioneered in 1927 by Filipino nationals from the United States, Vicente and Teodora DeFante. Rev. DeFante was converted at Angelus Temple and graduated from LIFE Bible College. The DeFantes were the first officially appointed Foursquare missionaries sent from the United States.

In 1930 George and Tony Illauan, also Filipino nationals, were sent from the United States. Both couples shared the gospel through house-to-house visitation and street meetings. Miracles of healing opened many doors to the gospel. As converts multiplied, leaders were trained and remained behind to follow up the new believers by teaching them the Word of God and establishing them in the faith. A national church began to develop as new "outstations" were started and churches were planted. In 1936 a national convention was held, and the major topic of discussion was how to evangelize Manila, the capital. The delegates concluded that beginning a central church in the capital would greatly facilitate the spread of the gospel throughout the country.

World War II delayed, but did not destroy, the implementation of the plan to penetrate the entire country. The first non-Filipino couples from the United States were sent following the war. The coming of the Al Chavezes, Everett Dennisons, Arthur Thompsons, Allan Hamiltons, Don McGregors, and Jack Richeys greatly strengthened and advanced the Foursquare work in the Philippines. In 1958 The Foursquare Church was organized into four districts. A missionary was assigned to each region to oversee church planting by national workers. New provinces began to open to the gospel as miracles attended the preaching of the Word. In addition to larger meetings, many home Bible studies became the avenues through which the gospel spread and through which entire families came to Christ. Within ten years the number of churches exceeded 200, and the number of members passed 10,000 as the work began to spread throughout the entire country. A researcher from another missions agency described the rapid expansion of the Foursquare work during this time as "New Testament fire in the Philippines."[6] Today The Foursquare Church in the Philippines is fully nationalized and has a constituency of more than 165,000 believers in more than 4,000 churches and meeting places. The gospel continues to spread as Foursquare workers evangelize in more than a dozen unreached groups in the Philippines and serve as missionaries in countries such as Japan and Papua New Guinea.

National church planting movements are taking place in other Asian countries such as Papua New Guinea, Sri Lanka, and Cambodia. These movements are significant since they are occurring in countries dominated by animistic and non-Christian religions such as Buddhism and Hinduism. Further, Foursquare work is beginning to show signs of taking root in several Muslim countries in Southeast Asia as well even though work among Muslims has been difficult. A Foursquare work was begun in Lebanon in 1962. But a civil war broke out in 1975 and forced the departure of most Foursquare members as well as the missionaries. However, new initiatives are taking place in the Middle East as well as in Central Asia with fellowships of believers now found in several nations.

Europe

In **Europe** there are encouraging signs of life and growth. Because Western Europe has not been viewed as a mission field and because the cost of supporting missionary personnel has been high, little was done to cultivate national church movements until recently. Although Foursquare work was initiated in the early 1930s in Greece, it was not until the 1980s that Western Europe became a focus for Foursquare missions. As a result there are indications that church planting movements are emerging in countries such as Spain, Switzerland, the Netherlands, Germany, and Greece. In Eastern Europe Foursquare is just beginning to develop ongoing initiatives in countries such as Croatia and Bulgaria. Meanwhile, ministry in the former Soviet Union, the Commonwealth of Independent States, has been taking place. Since much of the ministry has been largely unofficial, it is only in recent years that officially recognized Foursquare national works have begun to develop; the most recent of these is in Russia and Ukraine.

Conclusion

Over the past eight decades the Foursquare gospel has gone around the world. Today more than 6 million Foursquare believers meet in 50,000 fellowships in approximately 140 countries. With over 90 percent of these believers and fellowships outside North America, the Foursquare movement has truly become the *International* Church of the Foursquare Gospel. Over the past decade The Foursquare Church has had an average annual growth rate of nearly 10 percent. This means that it is doubling in size about every eight or nine years, winning an average of more than 4,000 people to Christ and planting five new churches every day.

The growth of the Foursquare movement has come in waves. The 1920s, the 1950s, the 1980s were all rapid periods of growth; additionally, the mid-1990s initiated a period of growth and expansion that has continued into the 21st century. As a result, the Foursquare movement has begun to see the need to identify more clearly and understand more fully its biblical and historic purpose, mission, and strategy. What has God blessed? How has He blessed it? Why has He blessed it? What has God so signally blessed since the inception of the Foursquare movement? It is evident that God has blessed the preaching of the gospel of Jesus Christ in the power of the Holy Spirit, the discipling of new believers in the ways of the Lord, and the establishing of strong local congregations in urban centers. How has God blessed such endeavors? He has confirmed the proclamation of the gospel with signs following and sinners repenting. He has blessed the making of disciples with believers growing and fruit remaining. He has honored the planting of local congregations with a multiplication of leaders and churches that have blossomed into national church movements. And why has God blessed such preaching, discipling, and planting? Because it fulfills His Son's commission to preach the gospel to every creature and make disciples of all nations. Furthermore, it honors and pleases God our Savior, "who wants all men to be saved and come to a knowledge of the truth [that] there is one God and one mediator between God and men, the man Christ Jesus who gave himself as a ransom for all men" (1 Timothy 2:4-6). This is the "story within the story." It's Luke's story, it's Foursquare's story, stories within "His story."

CHAPTER TWO

Disciples of All Nations:
National Church Development

Clarifying the Vision: Purpose, Mission, and Strategy

The process of clarifying the vision of The Foursquare Church's biblical purpose, historic mission, and practical strategy took a major step in the 1990s. After a two-year study the Foursquare Cabinet agreed upon the following statement.

Purpose: our reason for existence

The International Church of the Foursquare Gospel exists to glorify God and advance His kingdom in obedience to Jesus Christ's mandate to preach the gospel and make disciples of all nations/peoples (Mark 16:15; Matthew 28:19). Therefore, we are "Dedicated unto the cause of interdenominational and worldwide evangelism."

Mission: our assignment

In fulfillment of our biblical purpose we believe we are called to present Jesus Christ, God's Son, as "the Savior, the Healer, the Baptizer with the Holy Spirit and the coming King" and to establish healthy, mature, culturally appropriate, reproducing churches. Therefore, we are dedicated to the development of churches which are infinitely reproducible, making possible the continuous spread of the gospel to those yet unreached.

Strategy: our plan and goals

In order to fulfill its biblical purpose and historic mission the International Church of the Foursquare Gospel seeks to follow the pattern of Spirit-empowered church development found in the New Testament epistles and the book of Acts (Acts 1:8). Therefore, a four-stage developmental process is followed both in North America and throughout the world. Foursquare Missions focuses on such development internationally, seeking to foster a worldwide family of national churches related by loving servanthood.

An Infinitely Reproducible Pattern: A Life Cycle

Christ's call to "make disciples of all nations" requires an infinitely reproducible way of doing things. As we have seen, both the history of the Early Church in the first century and the history of the Foursquare movement in the twentieth century confirms the need for developing strong national church planting movements within cultures and countries. Such movements are infinitely reproducible, much like a life cycle.

Each stage in the cycle has the goal of reproducing what is infinitely reproducible. The goal of Stage 1 is to develop responsible disciples who reproduce disciples, becoming a local congregation. The goal of Stage 2 is to develop responsible leaders who reproduce leaders, edifying and equipping the congregation. The goal of Stage 3 is to develop responsible congregations that reproduce congregations, becoming a national movement. The goal of Stage 4 is to develop responsible national movements that send missionaries and reproduce other national movements, becoming an international movement. Such a pattern is infinitely reproducible and is somewhat like a wheel that continues to roll. More specifically, the process could be described in the following way:

Stage 1— from sinner to saint, from saint to obedient disciple of Jesus Christ

Stage 2— from obedient disciple to contributing member of the body of Christ, from contributing member to equipping leader in the body of Christ

Stage 3— from reproducing leader to church growth and expansion, from church expansion to church multiplication into a national movement

Stage 4—from church multiplication to cross-culture involvement, from cross-culture involvement to sending missionaries

...which initiates another national church movement cycle

Full development of a national church movement is similar to a life cycle, which moves through the stages of life from childhood to adolescence to young adult to older adult.

Like a *child*, the church is birthed by the Spirit and grows in the way of the Lord.

Like a *youth*, the church is nurtured and matures in unity and love.

Like a *young adult*, the church is fruitful and multiplies and gives birth to other churches.

Like an *older adult*, the church is supportive and sends workers to take the gospel to regions yet untouched with the gospel.

'The Foursquare cabinet has also approved the following amplification of the four-stage national church developmental process, believing it explains and illustrates how the International Church of the Foursquare Gospel is to continue to fulfill its biblical purpose and historic mission both in North America and around the world.[1]

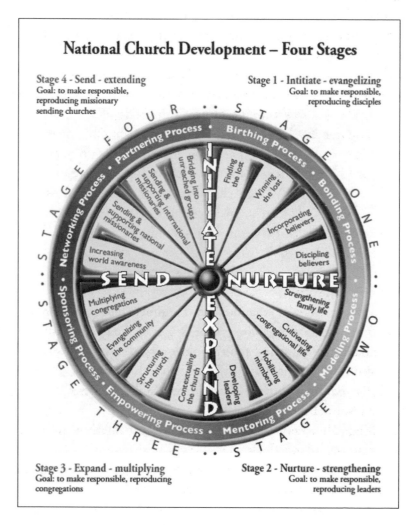

National Church Development – Four Stages

Stage 4 - Send - extending
Goal: to make responsible, reproducing missionary sending churches

Stage 1 - Intitiate - evangelizing
Goal: to make responsible, reproducing disciples

Stage 3 - Expand - multiplying
Goal: to make responsible, reproducing congregations

Stage 2 - Nurture - strengthening
Goal: to make responsible, reproducing leaders

Stage 1 - Initiate

We evangelize by winning the lost to Christ and by planting churches. The *goal* of Stage 1 is to make *responsible, reproducing disciples.* The task, therefore, is twofold. First, it requires communicating the gospel to people who are without Christ, the lost. Transferring believing church members from one church to another church is not evangelism. Rather, the lost must be sought, found, and won. Like Jesus' methods, the pattern is one of "go and tell" evangelism as well as "come and see" evangelism. Effective ways must be found to get the gospel *to* people. Then effective ways must be found to explain the gospel *for* people so that they can respond and make a meaningful decision concerning God's gracious offer of forgiveness of sin and eternal life based on the death and resurrection of Jesus Christ. The message is authenticated by both the lifestyle of believers showing the love of God and the presence of the miraculous that demonstrates the power of God. This gives the Holy Spirit the opportunity to convict of sin and give new birth, bringing about genuine conversion.

Second, the task of Stage 1 requires planting the church. As with a newborn child, the **birthing process** must be followed by the **bonding process**. Those who repent and believe the gospel must be openly identified with and warmly welcomed into the family of God. Therefore, in obedience to Christ's command, repentance and faith are to be followed by public confession in the waters of baptism and the receiving of the promised Holy Spirit as occurred on the Day of Pentecost. Beginning a local fellowship of believers is essential, for new converts need care and teaching. They need to be integrated into the family and taught to continue in obedience to all Christ commanded, thereby proving to be His disciples. Such responsible disciples will begin to reproduce themselves by winning their families and friends to the Savior. In the case of a pioneer situation, the sending church will seek to avoid incomplete strategies, namely, evangelizing without making disciples, making disciples without planting churches, or merely establishing a "token presence" in a region or country.

Stage 2 - Nurture

We strengthen the church by establishing sound doctrine and by training leaders. The *goal* of Stage 2 is to make *responsible, reproducing leaders.* Therefore, the task of this stage is also twofold. First, the developing of godly character is essential for a healthy church. The primary arena for shaping such Christ-like character is in the home, which is the church in its simplest and most original form. Here the soundness of doctrine can be put to the test. If the Christian faith is to become truly a part of the culture, it must be modeled by the parents and owned by the children. It must become multi-generational. Thus, parents, especially fathers, need to be trained to lead their families in the ways of the Lord. Since the church is in reality an extended family, the strengthening of family life is foundational to the cultivating of healthy congregational life.

Second, the task of Stage 2 requires training leaders. As with a maturing adolescent, the **modeling process** must be supplemented by the **mentoring process**. Training in maturity must be complemented by training in ministry. Growing up must result in giving out. Transforming takers into givers is the challenge. Because each member of the body of Christ has something to give, believers must be helped to identify, develop and use their divine giftedness for the good of others. Leaders, therefore, are gifted to serve, and they are gifted to equip others to do likewise. Such a releasing ministry is first seen in the home. Mobilizing people for the good of others is initially a family affair. Those who model servant-leadership and lead their families well are those who are to lead the body of Christ. Thus, emerging leaders are identified and developed so that the leadership base can be enlarged and the body of Christ edified and expanded. Making responsible, reproducing leaders is training leaders not only as leaders of followers but also as leaders of leaders. In Stage 2 leadership development and training are high priorities, aiding in increasing both the quantity and quality of leaders in anticipation of the type of expansion required for nationalization in Stage 3. In the case of a pioneer situation, the sending church will seek to avoid overuse of event-centered ministry, one-generational perspectives, edifice mentalities, rigid institutionalism, or excessive indebtedness.

Stage 3 - Expand

We multiply congregations within a region or nation by structuring for self-expression and self-government and by evangelizing through self-propagation and self-support. The *goal* of Stage 3 is to make *responsible, reproducing congregations* who multiply culturally appropriate churches that together become a regional or national church movement. Therefore, the task of Stage 3 is again twofold. First, it requires releasing the church in self-expression and self-government. A church must find a way to fit its environment so that it does not appear foreign and, thereby, erect unnecessary barriers to understanding and acceptance of the gospel. Its style of worship, fellowship, teaching, caring, and outreach must be appropriate to the culture in which it is ministering. Such contextualizing of ministry releases the church to serve its society more effectively and fruitfully. Further, the church must be structured in such a way as to release contextualized ministry. Form must follow and free function. Therefore, church government, organization, and administration should be kept simple, flexible, and practical, empowering the church to carry out its ministry in its community and culture.

Second, the task of Stage 3 requires multiplying into a regional or national movement through evangelizing its "Jerusalem" and multiplying churches in its "Judea." As with a growing young adult, the **empowering process** to help them "stand on their own two feet" must be complemented with the **sponsoring process** to give them meaningful opportunities to "try their wings." Expansion growth through winning the lost in its own culture requires a church to be involved in continual evangelism that is both sensitive and flexible. A combination of media, mass, and personal evangelistic methods will probably be necessary. Both programmed and spontaneous evangelism will be needed. This involves the witness of the corporate body of believers as well as the witness of individuals to family and friends within their sphere of influence. Extension growth through the starting of new churches within the larger region should follow. Like young adults, young congregations tend to be most reproductive within the first half of their life span. Church planting by local churches may need to be complemented by mobile apostolic type church planting teams that can pioneer churches at greater distances.[2] The development of appropriate regional structures will be essential. Where a sending church has been involved in pioneering another region or country, it will seek to provide affirming and freeing family-type relationships which avoid paternalism while retaining New Testament order. Further, it will seek to avoid politicizing or external ownership while the newly nationalized church will seek to avoid moving from Stage 1 to Stage 3 with inadequate focus on Stage 2.

Stage 4 - Send

We extend the church and advance the kingdom by sending and supporting missionaries and by bridging into other peoples, cultures and languages. The *goal* of Stage 4 is to make *responsible, reproducing missionary sending national churches* who make disciples of the nations in fulfillment of Christ's mandate. Therefore, the task of Stage 4 is twofold. First, it requires reaching nearby cultural groups. Many national churches have a blind spot when it comes to developing home missions outreaches among "Samaritans" who are culturally different but geographically near. Increasing awareness of the diversity of the world around them and its need for the gospel is best done initially through intercession. As people develop hearts of compassion, they will hear and respond when the Lord of the harvest begins to call laborers into his harvest. The national church will catch a vision and begin sending and supporting missionaries to culturally diverse groups within its own region and country.

Second, the task of Stage 4 requires reaching distant cultural groups in other countries, and is similar to an older adult who anticipates becoming a grandparent. The **networking process** of linking together those with common vision must be complemented by the **partnering process** of actually sharing together in a common task. Sending and supporting missionaries in another nation is a great challenge, especially when working among unreached groups. It frequently requires the expert counsel and the prayer and financial support of another national church. In some cases it may also require coordination and cooperation with missionaries from another national church who are also working within the same country. Sending churches will seek to avoid exporting their culture and methodologies or jumping from Stage 2 to Stage 4 with insufficient attention to Stage 3.

Conclusion

Analysis of the countries where The Foursquare Church is ministering indicates that each of the first three stages applies to 25-35 percent of the churches. Of the countries in Stage 1, many are in newly opened works. Some countries have been in this initial pioneering stage for years, indicating the need for additional training to move them into Stage 2. Stage 2 countries are established works. Again, some have been in this stage for years and need help to "stand on their own two feet" and develop strong national church planting movements. The Foursquare works in Stage 3 are becoming nationwide movements. Their next step is to catch and carry out a vision to fulfill the Great Commission among "all nations," including unreached ethnic groups within their own countries. Meanwhile 10-15 percent of overseas Foursquare works are Stage 4 churches. They have gone "full circle" and are sending and supporting both national and international missionaries. These non-Western "two-thirds world missionaries" are now pioneering Foursquare works in many of the newly opened countries.[3] These Stage 4 churches are those that participate in preaching the gospel of the kingdom "in the whole world as a witness to all nations...and then the end will come" (Matthew 24:14). These fully developed national churches are "full circle" churches that will keep the process of world evangelization "rolling" until Christ returns.[4] In the next four chapters we will take a closer look at each of these stages of "full circle" national church development.

CHAPTER THREE

Disciples of All Nations:
Stage One: Initiate—Evangelize

The initial stage is fundamental. Laying solid foundations is essential. As childhood is the first stage of the human life cycle and is the basis of all other stages, evangelism is the first phase of the life cycle of making disciples of all nations through national church development.

The goal of Stage 1 is to make responsible, reproducing disciples who continue to follow Christ. The task is twofold: communicating the gospel and beginning the church. It involves the birthing process, people being born again, and the bonding process, bringing them into the Body of Christ.

Communicating the Gospel: The Birthing Process

After His baptism in the Jordan River and the descent of the Spirit upon him, Jesus began to preach declaring, "The kingdom of God is near. Repent and believe the good news" (Mark 1:15). In the synagogue in his home town of Nazareth he read from the scroll of Isaiah: "The Spirit of the Lord is upon me, because he has anointed me to preach good news to the poor" (Isaiah 61:1). And what was the good news Jesus proclaimed? "Healing for the brokenhearted, freedom for prisoners, sight for the blind, release for the oppressed" (Luke 4:18, 19). He preached this good news of the kingdom of God throughout Galilee and Judea. Signs and wonders accompanied his preaching, for "God anointed Jesus of Nazareth with the Holy Spirit and power, and…he went around doing good and healing all who were under the power of the devil, because God was with him" (Acts 10:38).

Jesus communicated the gospel in word and deed. With authority and power he proclaimed and demonstrated the good news of the presence and power of God's kingdom to forgive, heal and deliver. He commissioned his disciples to do the same, sending them out to preach the message, "The kingdom of heaven (God) is near" and to "heal the sick, raise the dead, cleanse those who have leprosy, drive out demons" (Matthew 10:7, 8). Although initially sent "only to the lost sheep of Israel," Jesus, after his resurrection, commissioned his disciples to go and "make disciples of all nations." The Gospels record "all Jesus began to do and teach until the day he was taken up to heaven" (Acts 1:1). The Book of Acts tells the story of how the apostles and disciples continued to do what Jesus said and did, preaching the good news of the kingdom of God, healing the sick, and driving out demons. They "went out and preached everywhere, and the Lord worked with them and confirmed his word by the signs that accompanied it" (Mark 16:20). Likewise the Apostle Paul, persecutor turned preacher, fully proclaimed the gospel of Christ "in leading the Gentiles (nations) to obey God by what I have said and done—by the power of signs and miracles, through the power of the Holy Spirit" (Romans 15:18, 19). As did Jesus, His disciples communicated the good news of the God's kingdom in word and power, announcing God's offer of forgiveness and eternal life to all who would turn from their sins and put their trust in His Son, Jesus the Messiah.

Finding the lost

Why did Jesus come? He came to seek and to save that which was lost (Luke 19:10). He came to save sinners, to announce "the time of God's favor, the day of salvation" (2 Corinthians 6:2).

But what does it mean to be lost? In Luke 15 Jesus used three parables to describe "lostness." Lost people are like a lost sheep, a lost coin, a lost son. A lost sheep is helpless. It cannot save itself. It must be found and brought into the fold. This is why the shepherd will seek until he finds his one lost sheep. Jesus saw the multitudes as helpless and harassed, like sheep without a shepherd. Indeed, "all we like sheep have gone astray, each of us has turned to his own way" (Isaiah 53:6). Until the Good Shepherd finds us we are lost in sin, without God and without hope in this world. We cannot save ourselves. We need a Savior, a savior who will seek until he finds and saves us.

Lost people are like a lost coin. A lost coin is worthless. Though it may have the imprint of a famous ruler on it, it has no value. It is not until it is found and is back "in circulation" that it has worth. And so it was that the woman who lost the coin, perhaps a part of the dowry she would bring into a marriage, searched carefully until she found it. What is the value of one lost person? The whole world! For "what good is it for a man to gain the whole world, yet forfeit his soul? Or what can a man give in exchange for his soul?" (Mark 8:36, 37). We are valuable to God. We are worth finding and saving. We are made in His image. His imprint is stamped upon us. We belong to Him. We cannot find ourselves. We need a Savior, a savior who seeks until he finds.

Lost people are like a lost son. They are hopeless. Like a prodigal son they have left home, taking their father's gifts and foolishly spending them, ending up in a pig pen. Or they may be like an elder brother who, although he never left home, was just as lost. He was in the house but not of it. He was home alone, isolated and separated from his father's love, unable to enjoy the abundant life of a son. Likewise, we, having been given every good and perfect gift from the Father above, go our own way unrighteously squandering life in selfish pursuits like the younger brother, or like the elder brother self-righteously wallowing in self pity because we feel treated unfairly. But what love the Father has for all, whether unrighteous or self-righteous.

How he longs for us to know true life, abundant life, eternal life, that "everything he has is ours." But in contrast to a lost sheep and a lost coin, we can choose to be found, we can choose to return to the Father and enter into the joy of his house.

God's gift of salvation through his Son, Jesus Christ, is offered to all. "For God so loved the world that He gave His only Son, that whoever believes in him should not perish but have everlasting life" (John 3:16). This good news is to be communicated to everyone, for all have sinned and come short of God's glory. There is none righteous, not one. God did not send his Son into the world to condemn the world, but to save the world through him. Though condemned because of sin, God now offers forgiveness and life to all who turn from their sin and believe in his Son. Therefore, "whoever believes in the Son has eternal life, but whoever rejects the Son will not see life, for God's wrath remains on him" (John 3:36).

God does not want any to perish, but all to come to repentance (2 Peter 3:9). Because the wages of sin is death, through his death and resurrection Jesus Christ paid sin's penalty (death), defeated sin's author (Satan) and broke sin's power (the Law). Forgiveness and life, freedom and release, healing and hope are now offered through the gospel. And all who call on the name of the Lord will be saved—good news indeed!

But before the lost can be won to Christ, they must be found. Lost sheep, lost coins, and lost sons must be sought and found. That is why Jesus told us to "go," for "how can they hear without someone preaching to them? And how can they preach unless they are sent? As it is written, 'How beautiful are the feet of those who bring good news!'" (Romans 10:14, 15). And where are the lost to be found? Not in the fold! They are lost. It is in the finding and winning of the lost that the Kingdom of God is expanded and extended. We must find lost sheep, not transfer found sheep from fold to fold. Just as Jesus did, we too must have a passion to find what is lost: "other sheep that are not of this fold, they too must be brought in" (John 10:16).

Winning the lost

Jesus told his disciples that if they would follow him he would make them fishers of men (Matthew 4:19). In Jesus' day fishermen used nets, not poles, to catch fish. Andrew, Peter, James, and John were not sports fishermen; they were commercial fishermen. They netted fish, not hooked them. They caught many, not a few. The way Jesus "fished for men" and taught his disciples to fish is most instructive. His first followers were won through existing relationships. Andrew and Peter were brothers, James and John were brothers, and both sets of brothers were partners in a fishing business. In amazement they watched Jesus befriend a sinful Samaritan woman at a well, and, through her witness, scores of her friends and acquaintances came to believe in him (John 4:39-42). Like fish, people were found in "schools," in webs of relationships. These were the "nets" that frequently drew people to Jesus. Apparently the disciples learned how to fish like Jesus did, for the Book of Acts records that many came to Christ, including whole households such as that of Cornelius, Lydia, the Philippian jailer and the Jewish rabbi, Crispus. Whole villages turned to the Lord as well as religious and social groups.[1] The same is true today. More people come to Christ through existing relationships with family, friends, acquaintances, and neighbors than any other way. Such existing spheres of influence are the primary "fishing ponds" in winning people the lost to Christ, then and now.[2]

This good news of forgiveness of sin and reconciliation to God through Christ must be communicated to the lost. At the heart of the gospel is the communication of Christ's death and resurrection and their redemptive meaning. Yes, Christ died and was buried. But why? It was for our sins (1 Corinthians 15:3-5). Yes, Christ rose from the dead and was seen by witnesses. But why? It was for our justification, that we might be put right with God (Romans 4:25). This is the good news that must be preached to the lost. God so loved the world so much he gave his only son so that whoever believes and receives him should not perish in eternal lostness, but have eternal life.

Accompanying evangelism must be good deeds. Good works need to accompany good news. People need to hear the gospel, but they also need to see it. Jesus said that his followers are "the light of the world and the salt of the earth." Therefore, we are to "let our light so shine before men that they may see our good works and glorify our Father in heaven" (Matthew 5:16).

The love of God in Christ is not only expressed in word, but in deed—practical deeds of kindness and acts of compassion—caring for the needy, healing the sick, delivering the bound, helping the poor, feeding the hungry, seeking justice for the oppressed, and meeting the needs orphans and widows. Hungry stomachs have no ears. Jesus went about "doing good." Moved with compassion, he fed the multitudes, healed the sick, cast out demons as he preached good news to the poor. The Early Church did likewise. In the words of the Apostle Paul, "as we have opportunity, let us do good to all people, especially those who belong to the family of believers" (Galatians 6:10).

In more under-evangelized and resistant cultures, such good works may need to precede and prepare the soil for the communication of the good news of the gospel. As has been said, "People do not care how much you know until they know how much you care." The communication of the good news of the kingdom is in word and deed, in deeds both supernatural and natural, both miraculous and merciful. Moved by compassion we heal the sick, help the needy, and preach good news to the poor.[3]

Seeking and saving, finding and winning people to Christ will take time. Evangelism is a process. There are different types of soil: hard, stony, thorny and soft (Mark 4:1-10), and there are different seasons for working the soil: plowing, sowing, cultivating, and reaping. Between the planting of the seed and the reaping of the harvest there is a process that requires time, time for the seed to grow, develop, and ripen. Between the planting of the seed of the gospel and the harvest "unto eternal life" there frequently is a period of time. Just as there is a gestation period between conception and physical birth, there seems to be a "gestation period" for spiritual birth.

Most people come to Christ through a process. Some may come to salvation more quickly than others, but all go through a process of hearing, understanding, reflecting, accepting, and believing the gospel. How long did it take for Andrew, Peter, James, and John to believe? And what of Nicodemus and Joseph of Arimethea? And what about Jesus' own brothers, James and Jude, who apparently did not believe until after his resurrection? [4]

Frequently the length of the process depends on the receptivity of an individual or even a group. How open are they to hear? How ready are they to respond? Do they have ears to hear, a heart to believe? Why is some soil hard, while other soil is soft? Not all soil is the same. Jesus recognized this reality. He told the Twelve that, when they entered a town or village, to "search for some worthy person there and stay at his house until you leave." However, "if anyone will not receive you or listen to your words, shake the dust off your feet when you leave that home or that town" (Matthew 10:11, 14). Why were some communities like Capernaum more open to receive Jesus than others, like Nazareth and Chorazin? Why were "sinners" such as prostitutes and tax collectors more receptive than the Sadducees and Pharisees? But seasons change, and hearts soften. How many of the 3,000 who believed on the Day of Pentecost were among those who had shouted for the death of Jesus two weeks earlier? And how many more were among multiple thousands of Jews who believed within the next several months (Acts 4:4)? Why was it that even from resistant religious leaders "a large number of priests became obedient to the faith" (Acts 6:7)?

Resistant, or apparently resistant, individuals and groups must not be neglected. They too must be sought and found, but it may take more time for them to respond. While the focus may be on the more receptive, the resistant can and do respond in time. Watered by prayer, softened by circumstances, confronted by crisis, drawn by deeds of kindness, the less responsive can be brought to Christ in due season.

But whatever the length of time it takes for a person to understand and respond in repentance from sin and faith in Jesus Christ, all must be born again, for Jesus himself said: "Unless one is born again (*anothen*, "from above"), he cannot see the kingdom of God" (John 3:3). Just as a person must be "born of the flesh" (physically) to enter the human family, so a person must be "born of the Spirit" (from above) to enter God's family (John 3:5-7).

Finding and Winning the Lost

When U.S. missionaries Ted and Sou Olbrich arrived in Cambodia in 1999, there was one Foursquare church. Today there are nearly 2,000 churches and meeting places and more than 150,000 members. Believing the church must be proactive and holistic in communicating the gospel, love for the total person, spirit, soul and body is being demonstrated. The gospel is proclaimed in the power of the Spirit with the sick being healed and the bound delivered. Believers are being trained in Christian truth, and "called" leaders are equipped and sent to plant new churches. Socially, the gospel is demonstrated by teaching family values; strengthening family structure; feeding, housing and training orphans; and assisting widows. Materially, the gospel is shown by providing clothes and food to the needy and assisting them to establish self-sustaining agricultural enterprises and training city dwellers in micro-enterprise opportunities. More than one hundred Foursquare Children of Promise church/orphan homes have been established, and they house, feed, and train more than 4,000 orphans who are cared for by widows. These locations serve as local churches as well and reach out to their surrounding areas. They also serve as divisional headquarter churches and training centers for the Foursquare movement in Cambodia.

Beginning the Church: the Bonding Process

The initial "birthing process" of communicating the gospel involves finding and winning the lost to Christ. The second phase of Stage 1 is the "bonding process." Just as a newborn baby bonds to the mother and is brought into a family, so the newborn child of God must be connected and brought into the family of God. Although we have only two references of Jesus speaking about the Church (Matthew 16:18; 18:17), the proclamation of the gospel in the Book of Acts resulted in the establishing of churches throughout the Roman Empire. Those who believed were consistently incorporated into the Body of Christ, the local fellowship of believers called "the church" (*ekklesia*: "called out ones"). A fellowship of believers is essential within which newborn believers can be taught, nurtured, and strengthened in the faith. Newborns, whether physical or spiritual, need families in order to survive and thrive. They need to be brought into a family and trained how to live in a family. Thus the "bonding process" is twofold: incorporating new believers and discipling them in the ways Jesus Christ, their Lord.

Incorporating new believers

Jesus promised his disciples, "You will receive power when the Holy Spirit comes on you; and you will be my witnesses in Jerusalem, and in all Judea and Samaria, and to the ends of the earth" (Acts 1:8). When the Holy Spirit came upon them on the Day of Pentecost, it was Peter who stood up with the Eleven and preached the good news about Jesus Christ. He boldly declared that a new day had dawned: "This is that." The outpouring of the Spirit signaled the "last days" when "whoever calls on the name of the Lord will be saved" (Acts 2:17-21). Peter clearly proclaims this Jesus of Nazareth, who "you, with the help of wicked men, put him to death by nailing him to the cross" God has now raised from the dead and "we are all witnesses of the fact" (Acts

2:23, 32). Furthermore, "exalted to the right hand of God, he has received of the Father the promised Holy Spirit and has poured out what you now see and hear" (Acts 2:33). Therefore, Peter concludes, "God has made this Jesus, whom you crucified, both Lord and Christ" (Acts 2:36). Jesus of Nazareth is both Master and Messiah. He is the Savior upon whom all are to call and be saved.

When the people heard this, they were "cut to the heart" and asked, "What shall we do?" Peter replied: "Repent, be baptized and receive the gift of the Holy Spirit." He further pleaded with them, "Save yourselves from this corrupt generation," and about 3,000 accepted the message, were baptized, and were added to their number on the Day of Pentecost (Acts 2:38-41). Throughout the Book of Acts this appears to be the pattern of beginning life with Christ and entering the family of God: repent and believe in Christ, be baptized and receive the gift of the Holy Spirit.[5] The initial "making of a disciple" is done through the public identification with Christ in the waters of baptism and the receiving of the gift of the Holy Spirit. This is how new believers were incorporated into the Church, the Body of Christ, beginning with the Day of Pentecost. To be identified with Christ is to be identified with his body. As with marriage, so it is with baptism—the public ceremony confirms and seals the uniting of a man and a woman not only to each other but also to each other's family.

Discipling believers

With children, the goal is to train them to walk, talk, feed themselves, and obey. And such training takes place within a family. So it is with disciples who are to be taught to walk in the ways of the Lord and to obey all Christ commanded (Matt. 28:20). The training of Jesus' disciples took place in the context of personal relationships. Jesus called the Twelve that they "might be with him" before sending them out (Mark 6:14). He taught and trained his disciples just as parents teach and train their children, within the context familial relationships. Jesus discipled the Twelve in the family setting of a "small group," which after Pentecost would frequently be within the context of the home.

The first step in "obeying all that Jesus commanded" is water baptism. Jesus instructed his disciples to begin the making of disciples by baptizing them in the name of the Father, Son, and Holy Spirit" (Matthew 28:19).[6] In so doing, those who believed were identified both with Christ in his death and resurrection and with his body, the fellowship of followers of like faith.

Following the Day of Pentecost those who believed devoted themselves to the apostles' teaching, to fellowship, to the breaking of bread, and to prayer (Acts 2:42). Though the number of believers was large, it was in the context of familial relationships that the apostles taught. Luke records that "all the believers were together and had everything in common… every day they continued to meet together in the temple courts…they broke bread in their homes and ate together with glad and sincere hearts praising God and enjoying the favor of all the people" (Acts 2:44-46).

And what did the apostles teach? What they had been taught by Jesus, what we have recorded in the Gospels. And of all the Gospels, Matthew appears to arrange and summarize most clearly what Jesus taught in "teaching blocks." Five times in his Gospel he concludes a teaching section with the phrase "when Jesus had finished saying these things."[7] Like children, these earliest believers needed practical life-related teaching so they might know and do the will of the Father. The twelve practical subjects in the Sermon on the Mount in Matthew 5-7, the first of the five teaching sections, are an example of what Jesus taught his disciples about the will of the Father in heaven.[8] True disciples continue in Christ's word, hearing and doing what he commanded (John 8:31-34). In so doing they build their lives upon a sure foundation. Jesus said, "Everyone who hears these words of mine and puts them into practice is like a wise man, who built his house upon the rock" and when "the rain came down, the streams rose, and the winds blew and beat against that house…it did not fall down because it had its foundation on the rock" (Matthew 7:24, 25).

And so the earliest believers were taught what Jesus taught his disciples. After Pentecost they "devoted themselves to the apostles' teaching" (Acts 2:42). As the Twelve became disciples of Jesus by learning to obey what he commanded, they likewise made disciples, training believers by exhortation and example to become true followers of Jesus Christ. As they had been discipled, so they discipled new believers, and in so doing began an infinitely reproducible process that continues to this day—disciples of Jesus Christ making disciples until disciples are made of all nations.

Incorporating and Discipling New Believers

In the early years of the work in Panama, a strong youth program discipled and incorporated young people into the life of the church. A majority of these young people were new believers. As a youth society, the program had its own leadership committee, with an advisor designated by the local pastor. The youth set the agenda, including a Sunday evening service an hour before the evening service. Amazingly the youth did everything the adults did. They ushered, played instruments, led worship, preached brief messages, and counseled new converts. The program was modeled after the adult service but had multiple preachers. Ministry was not confined to the church building. Weekly outreach included handing out tracts in different parts of Panama City. Leaders emerged from these youth services and outreaches, and many later became key pastors of the Foursquare church. Leadership was taught through responsibility. When asked the end result of this youth movement, missionary Leland Edwards responded, "They had a burden to reach their country for Christ!"

Conclusion

We have seen that a national church movement begins with a passion for evangelism. This passion comes by the working of the Spirit through whom the love of God is shed abroad in our hearts (Romans 5:5). It is the love of Christ that constrains us (2 Corinthians 5:14). Finding and winning lost sheep...Jesus did it. We do it. As long as there are sheep that are not yet of His fold, they too must be sought and saved (John 10:16).

When lost sheep are found, they must be brought into the fold, connected to God's family. They must be cared for, fed, and taught the ways of the Good Shepherd so they can become strong and reproductive disciples of him. A national movement not only begins with a passion for evangelism. It is sustained by it. Stage 1 continues throughout all the other stages. Seeking and winning lost sheep, bringing them into the fold and discipling them is always in season.

CHAPTER FOUR

Disciples of All Nations:
Stage Two: Nurture—Strengthen

Introduction

The second stage of a life cycle is adolescence, or youth, when a growing child becomes a young person who is maturing, learning how to relate to others, and assuming responsibility. In the life of a church, it is the stage when the fellowship and life together of believers is established, strengthened, and nurtured. It is fundamental in the development of subsequent stages. The goal of Stage 2 is to make responsible, reproducing leaders. The task is twofold: developing godly character and releasing fruitful ministry, a modeling and mentoring process.

Developing Godly Character: The Modeling Process

Jesus is our model. The Father seeks sons and daughters who will reflect the likeness of his only begotten Son in whom he is well pleased. In everything God "works for the good of those who love him, who have been called according to his purpose...to be conformed to the likeness of his Son" (Romans 8:28, 29). As God's children we are called to live a godly, Christ-like life of love and holiness in two primary arenas, the home and the church. The development of godly character in both the home and the church takes place as parents and leaders model Christ-like liv-

ing. This requires the strengthening of family life and the cultivating of healthy congregational life.

Strengthening family life

God planned the family, and it is the first institution he created.
It reflects his relationship with humankind as creator (Malachi
2:10), and more significantly it reflects his intended relationship
as redeemer (Isaiah 63:7-9)—a father and his family. The family
is foundational. The home is the place where children are shaped
and molded most consistently and effectively. It is God's primary
laboratory for cultivating spiritual life, growth, and maturity.

God made people in his image, male and female (Genesis
1:27). Although God also made animals male and female, they do
not marry. However, when a man "leaves his father and mother
and is united to his wife…they become one flesh" (Genesis 2:24).
This unity in marriage reflects the unity of God himself. The
word "one" used to describe the unity of husband and wife is the
same word used to describe the unity, the oneness of God in
Deuteronomy 6:4. It is interesting to note that the word that
describes marital and divine "oneness" is *echad* not *yachid*, the
word used of Abraham's offering of his "one and only" son
(Genesis 22:2). The focus is unity rather than singularity.

Further, in the Old Testament God's relationship to his peo-
ple is described as that of a husband and wife (Jeremiah 3:14;
Hosea 2:16). In the New Testament Christ's relationship to his
Church is described as that of a bridegroom and bride
(Ephesians 5:31, 32). Marriage models a "oneness" that is true of
God's own nature and his relationship with his people, a loving
unity. And it is in this relationship of God with His people, of
Christ's relationship with his Church, that the true meaning of
the relationship of a husband and wife is discovered and nurtured. By learning to love his wife as Christ loved the Church,
the husband models the way of servant leadership. By learning to
trust and follow her husband as the Church trusts and follows

Christ, the wife models the way of liberating submission (Ephesians 5:21-30).

Just as Christ's example of love and submission is the model for marriage, so the relationship between a husband and a wife is a key to raising godly children. As the husband and wife learn to model Christ-likeness in their relationship, the children learn to trust, obey, respect, and honor their father and mother just as their parents trust, obey, respect, and honor the Lord. Instead of provoking their children, parents are to raise them in the discipline and instruction of the Lord, encouraging them to follow their example as they follow the example of Christ (1 Corinthians 11:1). In this way the faith of the parents is passed on and owned by the next generation. Godly character as evidenced by Christ-like living and the fruit of the Spirit is best nurtured in the home where life is lived day in and day out and its most fundamental relationships worked out. Home is where learning to love God and one another takes place best. Such nurturing of healthy and strong marital and family relationships is one of the primary ways Jesus builds his Church. And so it is that a church, in its simplest and most biblical form, that of a family, begins to take root and bear fruit in a culture.[1]

Cultivating healthy congregational life

A church is, in a sense, an "extended family of families." Just as a Christian family is strengthened and established, so a church is strengthened and established. Healthy families make for healthy churches, churches characterized by a sense of community and loving unity.

In the Early Church the sense of family was evident as they devoted themselves to teaching, fellowship, the breaking of bread and prayer (Acts 2:42). Regularly they met together in the temple courts and "broke bread in their homes, eating together with glad and sincere hearts" (Acts 2:46).[2] Genuine community developed as "all the believers (young and old) were together and had everything in common…giving to anyone as he had need" (Acts 2:44, 45). The Church functioned as an intergenerational family. Although they did not live communally, they functioned as a community. There were "no needy persons among them, for from time to time those who owned lands or houses sold them, brought the money from the sales and put it at the apostles feet and it was distributed to anyone as he had need" (Acts 4:34, 35). Such sharing was voluntary. It was not required or forced. It was the work of the Spirit in the hearts of believers nourishing the "grace of giving." They discovered the truth in the words of Jesus that it is "more blessed to give than to receive" (Acts 20:35).[3]

Such a community spirit of love and care continued and expanded. Some years later the prediction of famine occasioned the providing of help for the brothers living in Judea, and the disciples in Antioch gave according to their ability (Acts 11:27-30). At times even poorer churches such as those in Macedonia asked if they could share in such "service to the saints" (2 Corinthians 8:1-5). Using the example of Jesus himself who, "though he was rich, yet for you sakes became poor, so that you through his poverty might be made rich" (2 Corinthians 8:9), the Apostle Paul encouraged the church at Corinth to "excel in this grace of giving." He was not advocating that others be relieved while they were hard pressed. Rather, appealing to the biblical principle of equality (Exodus 16:18), he encouraged them to allow their abundance to supply the need of others, for the day could come when they may be in need of the supply of other saints (2 Corinthians 8:13-15). Meeting the needs of the family of God, the Body of Christ, is love working by faith. It is the love by which Jesus himself said, "All men will know you are my disciples" (John 13:35).

Such a community of caring and sharing is essential in cultivating healthy congregational life. Through loving unity the congregation's spiritual life, growth, and maturity flourish. The Apostle Paul exhorted the Ephesians to "make every effort to keep the unity of the Spirit in the bond of peace" (Ephesians

4:3), for it is where God's people learn to "live together in unity...[that] the Lord bestows his blessing, even life forevermore" (Psalm 133:1-3). Such heaven-born unity of the Spirit is a reality to be maintained and lived out. Children born of the same earthly parents are to live out the reality of their common life by loving one another.

So it is in the family of God. There is but *one body* created by *one Spirit* called to *one hope*. There is but *one Lord* and *one faith* confessed in *one baptism*. There is but *one God* and Father of all who have been born into his family (Ephesians 4:4-6). These seven "ones" are the realities that are the basis of life together in the Body of Christ. Therefore, Paul exhorts followers of Christ to "live a life worthy of the calling you have received, being completely humble and gentle, patient and bearing with one another in love" (Ephesians 5:1, 2). As God's "dearly loved children" we are called to be "imitators of God...and live a life of love, just as Christ loved us and gave himself for us" (Ephesians 5:1, 2). In learning so to live, the community of believers is expressing the unity that characterizes God himself. They are one as the Father and Son are one. And such love and unity of heart and mind, Jesus said, "lets the world know that you sent me and have loved them even as you have loved me" (John 17:23). This witness of loving unity was Christ's last request to his Father before he died.

It is in a loving and caring community the sense of the presence of God is evident. It is here God's people unitedly and openly worship, freely give, and humbly serve each other whenever and wherever they meet, whether in large or small gatherings. Together they pray for one another, confess their sins to one another, and forgive one another. Together they instruct one another; stir up one another; submit to one another; and speak to one another with psalms, hymns and spiritual songs, singing and making music in their hearts to the Lord as they sincerely love one another from the heart.[4] In its simplest form the gathered community of believers, the Church, is where "Christ is all and in all" (Colossians 3:11). He is central and preeminent over all. He is resident and present in all. No wonder his presence and love are evident and resident.

Strengthening Family Life and Cultivating Congregational Life

Convinced that the family is God's idea and the basic unit to represent His love, provision, and care of its members, Marc and Kathy Shaw pioneered a church in their home near Frankfurt, Germany. Committed to remain close and strong as a family, they wanted the church to have the same sense of family, intergenerational and relational, but without sacrificing the primary mission of reaching the lost. As the Frankfurt church grew, this focus on the family continued to characterize this congregation, and it characterized the daughter and granddaughter churches born out of this fellowship as well. Although the church eventually outgrew the house, it never outgrew the sense of family, not even into the second and third generation of churches. With a focus on small group ministry and discipleship, even with service teams, the "DNA" of family continued. Today the Foursquare Church in Germany has grown to more than thirty churches.

Releasing Ministry: The Mentoring Process

The distinguishing mark of the believer is the presence of the Holy Spirit. It is those who have the Spirit of Christ that belong to him (Romans 8:9). In contrast to the unbeliever who is devoid of the Spirit, those who have placed their trust in Christ are the temple, or dwelling place, of the Holy Spirit "who is in you, whom you have received from God" (1 Corinthians 6:19). Because we were all "baptized by one Spirit into one body...and all given the one Spirit to drink" (1 Corinthians 12:13), every member of the body of Christ is important and necessary. To each one the manifestation of the Spirit is given for the common good. Therefore, the development and release of each member's gift and ability are essential to build up and strengthen the church. This is accomplished in two ways: equipping members and developing leaders. In both these arenas, the mentoring and training of members and leaders is a key in releasing ministry in and through the church in the community

Equipping members

Like our physical body, every member is different by divine design. Each has a distinct and important function. When all the members of the Body of Christ work together in unity with a common purpose, they build each other up and exalt Jesus Christ. The result is health and growth. The gifts of the risen Christ to his Church are apostles, prophets, evangelists, pastors and teachers (Ephesians 4:11). Each of these gifted leaders is given to equip the saints for serving so that the Body of Christ may be built up and become mature, united in the faith and the knowledge of God's Son, measuring up to the fullness of Christ himself (Ephesians 4:16).

All these leaders Christ has given to the Church are both servants and equippers of the Body of Christ. They themselves not only serve but also equip others to serve. Apostles are *ambassadors* called and sent of God to begin and establish the Church. They also equip God's people for works of service in guiding and putting in order the Body of Christ. Prophets are *messengers* of God called and anointed to communicate His will and word. They also equip believers in understanding and speaking His message to build up, lift up and stir up the Church to love and good works. Evangelists are *proclaimers* of good news called and gifted to share the gospel with unbelievers. They also equip believers to be faithful witnesses of Christ in their homes and community. Pastors are *shepherds* who are called and set apart by God to lead and feed the flock of God. They also equip the people of God in nurturing and caring for the sheep of His pasture. Teachers are *interpreters* of God's Word who are called and appointed to communicate truth and sound doctrine that lead to holy living and good works. Teachers also equip God's people by wise instruction and practical teaching. Such equipping is in word and deed, both by exhortation and example. In the words of the Apostle Paul, "Whatever you have learned or received or heard from me, or seen in me—put it into practice" (Philippians 4:9).

As gifted leaders and equippers, apostles, prophets, evangelists, pastors and teachers help the members of the Body of Christ to identify, stir up and use the gifts and abilities God has given them to do the work of ministry. Whether gifts of speaking (prophecy, teaching, exhortation, word of wisdom, word of knowledge, tongues, interpretation of tongues), gifts of helping (giving, showing mercy, helps, service, hospitality), gifts of power (faith, healings, miracles), gifts of seeing (discernment) or gifts of leading (governments), all are for the building up the Body of Christ.[5] As each member does its part, the whole body grows and builds itself up in love (Ephesians 4:16). This "synergy of the Spirit" brings about the kind of maturity where God's people are "no longer infants, tossed back and forth by the waves and blown here and there by every wind of teaching…instead, speaking the truth in love, [they] will in all things grow up into him who is the Head, that is, Christ" (Ephesians 4:14, 15).

Developing servant-leaders

The home is the primary place of spiritual nurture and growth, and it is also the primary place of leadership development. Those who lead well in their homes are those who are able to lead in the family of God. The Apostle Paul gave clear instructions to both Timothy (1 Timothy 3:1-13) and Titus (Titus 1:5-9) concerning the selection of leaders in the Body of Christ. Among the primary qualifications were marital fidelity and family order. "An elder must be blameless, the husband of but one wife, a man whose children believe and are not open to the charge of being wild and disobedient" (Titus 1:6). "He must manage his own family well and see that his children obey him with proper respect, [for] if anyone does not know how to manage his own family, how can he take care of God's church" (1 Timothy 3:4, 5). And such qualifications applied not only to elders or overseers, but to deacons as well for they "must be the husband of but one wife and must manage his children and household well" (1 Timothy 3:12).[6] It was from such leaders whose lives modeled Christ-like qualities that apostles, prophets, evangelists, pastors, and teachers came (Ephesians 4:11).

Of the qualifications of those who lead, only one had to do with ability ("able to teach," 1 Timothy 3:2). All others had to do with quality of character, such as attitudes, priorities, habits, reputation and maturity.[7] Skills were important, but character was primary, for leadership in the Body of Christ is as much about who we are as it is about what we do. Therefore, God's leaders must be above reproach (*anenkeltos*, "not open to censure, blameless," 1 Timothy 3:2) who, by their Christ-like lives, confirm that they truly know the God they serve.

Jesus is not only our example for living but also our model for leading. He came not "to be served, but to serve and to give his life a ransom for many" (Mark 10:45). His style of leadership was that of a servant. On several occasions when his disciples were jealously vying for position, Jesus described the way to achieve true greatness in the kingdom of God. He told his followers, "Whoever wants to become great among you must be your servant (*diakonos*), and whoever wants to be first must be slave (*doulos*) of all" (Mark 10:44; cp. 9:33-35). At the conclusion of the Last Supper on the eve of his death, a dispute again arose as to who was the greatest (Luke 22:24-27). "I am among you as one who serves," Jesus reminded them. Apparently it was at this point he began to wash the disciples' feet (John 13:1-17). He concluded that servant's task with these words: "I have set you an example that you should do as I have done for you. I tell you the truth, no servant is greater than his master, nor is a messenger greater than the one who sent him. Now that you know these things, you will be blessed if your do them" (John 13:15-17). And do them they did. The Book of Acts described those who led the Church as faithfully proclaiming the Word, and also feeding and caring for the flock of God and "not lording it over those entrusted to (them), but being examples to the flock" (1 Peter 5:3). Servant leadership characterized the Early Church and was evident in the lives of apostles, such as Peter and John (2 Peter 1:1; Revelation 1:1); elders, such James and Jude (James 1:1; Jude 1:1); and the seven who were called to serve (*diakonein*) tables, such the Stephen and Philip (Acts 6:3-6).

Those who led well first in their homes and then in the Church modeled Christ-like leadership. As good and faithful servants, even if young, they became like Timothy, "an example for the believers" in word and deed (1 Timothy 4:12). Stirring up the gifts given to them by the Spirit, they devoted themselves to the ministry of the Word in preaching and teaching, learning to "watch their life and doctrine closely" (1 Timothy 4:13-16). They taught both the older and the younger men and women. They encouraged the older to teach the younger those things that are in accord with sound doctrine by being devoted to good works so that "in every way they will make the teaching about God our Savior attractive" (Titus 2:1-10). Thus, as the ministry of teaching and living sound doctrine was expanded, the witness of Christ was extended. Paul urged Timothy to entrust the things he had heard him say in the presence of many witnesses to "reliable men who will also be qualified to teach others" (2 Timothy 2:2). Paul taught Timothy, who taught other reliable men, who were commissioned to teach others the truths they had received. Such multiplication of leaders who teach others to teach others is essential to the growth and expansion of the Church; it is a key to maturity and multiplication.

Mobilizing Members and Developing Leaders

When missionaries left Sri Lanka in 1981, Leslie and Belen Keegel were appointed as national leaders. Although the nation has been torn by civil war over the past two decades, the Foursquare work has grown through the planting of house churches; today there are more than 1,000 churches throughout the nation. As home churches develop, especially in urban centers, the groups often become established churches. These "center churches" serve as bases from which workers are mobilized, trained, and deployed, establishing new groups across the country. Pastors are trained and equipped through a Bible institute and In-service Leadership Training (ILT) seminars. It is through ILT seminars many leaders receive their initial training in ministry; they gather every three to four months in an urban center for two- to three-week leadership training intensives based on a core curriculum of twelve basic ILT courses in Bible, theology, and ministry. Out of these seminars a Bible institute was developed for training and equipping younger emerging leaders who are being discipled and mentored by their pastors. Such ongoing multiplication of leaders has been a key in the continuing growth and expansion of the Foursquare work throughout Sri Lanka, even during a time of increasing persecution and civil unrest.

Conclusion

The making of disciples of all nations starts with evangelism and beginning a church, and is both a birthing and bonding process. Its goal is the making of responsible, reproducing disciples. The second stage nurtures what is initiated in the first stage. It involves strengthening the church by developing godly character and releasing ministry, a modeling and mentoring process. Its goal is the making of responsible reproducing leaders. Through the strengthening of family life and the cultivating of healthy congregational life, followers of Jesus Christ are formed and transformed into his likeness. Through equipping members of the Body of Christ for the work of ministry and the developing of servant leaders the church grows up, grows together, grows more and grows out.

CHAPTER FIVE

Disciples of All Nations:
Stage Three: Expand—Multiply

Introduction

The third stage of a life cycle is young adult, when most people leave parents, marry, establish a home, and have children. It is the season of life when reproduction and multiplication take place. This is the stage when a congregation that has been fruitful in making disciples and training leaders begins to multiply and becomes a movement that can touch a nation. The goal of Stage 3 is the making of responsible, reproducing congregations. The task is twofold: empowering the church to be released and grow, and sponsoring the church to multiply and expand.

Releasing the Church to Grow: The Empowering Process

Young adults are prepared and released to establish their own families. Likewise, the young church is to be prepared and released to be fruitful and multiply in its own culture and country. The church must be empowered, that is, given the responsibility and authority to develop without continual dependence on outside help. This takes place in two ways: by contextualizing the life and ministry of the church and by structuring the church to release growth.

Contextualizing the Church

If a church is be fruitful and multiply, it must fit the setting in which it is ministering. It has to be released to develop in a way that is culturally appropriate so that it can become truly indigenous. It needs to express, lead, support, and multiply itself without undue outside assistance or continual dependence. Like a newly married couple establishing their home, a young church must be prepared and allowed to "stand on its own two feet" and "try its wings."

One of the first areas of helping a church contextualize and "fit" its environment is by empowering it to express itself in biblically valid and personally authentic ways of faith and practice. What are the biblical essentials of faith in Christ? How should they be lived out? How shall "the faith once delivered to the saints" (Jude 3) be explained and expressed in the culture?[1]

The New Testament letters are prime examples of such a clarification and application of the gospel in a first century setting. Listen to the words of the apostle Peter at the end of his first epistle. "I have written to you briefly, encouraging and testifying that this is the true grace of God. Stand fast in it" (1 Peter 5:12). He explained to his readers the faith they had believed ("the true grace of God") and exhorted them to practice it ("stand fast in it"). The Apostle Paul did likewise in Romans. "In light of God's mercy, I urge you to offer your bodies as living sacrifices, holy and pleasing to God which is your spiritual worship" (Romans 12:1). In the first eleven chapters Paul clearly explained the gospel, which is the power of God to save all who believe, whether Jew or Gentile. Having shown that none are righteous, no not one, and that all have fallen short of the glory of God, Paul explained how God has "bound all men over to disobedience so that he may have mercy on them all" (Romans 11:32), for in the gospel is revealed "a righteousness from God which is by faith from first to last" (Romans 1:16, 17).

In light of such amazing grace and mercy, Paul answered the

question, "How then shall we who have believed live?" Living the life of faith, Paul explained, means not being confirmed to the pattern of this world but being transformed by the renewing of your mind so you can test and approve what God's will is in serving the Body of Christ, submitting to governing authorities, building up those weak in faith and maintaining a spirit of unity (Romans 12-15). Explaining and living the gospel in the first century Roman world was a matter of the "contextualization of the faith" in word and deed.

How can the follower of Jesus Christ be in the world but not of it? How can a church authentically express the true grace of God in its culture and country without falling into a syncretism that dilutes the gospel and without developing a foreignness that warps the gospel? How can it avoid the extremes of over-contextualization that allows culture to overwhelm the gospel, and under-contextualization, which results in a reluctance to engage culture?

Empowering a church with the responsibility and authority to discover how to authentically express and personally practice its faith is essential if it is going to become truly indigenous. The truth of the gospel remains the same, but patterns and practices vary from culture to culture. This was true in the first century. How Gentile believers in Rome worshiped, fellowshipped, and lived out their Christian faith was probably different than that of Jewish believers in Jerusalem. But all were members of the same family, the family of God, the Body of Christ. And so it is today. The way Caucasian believers in North American worship, fellowship, and live out their faith is different from Latin American believers in South America, is different from African believers in sub-Saharan Africa, and is different from South Asian believers in India. As one Indian evangelist said, "Don't bring the Gospel as a potted plant. Bring it as seed and plant it in Indian soil and let it grow." The seed of the gospel is the same because Jesus is the same yesterday, today, and forever, but the cultural soil varies. God sent His Son in the fullness of time to be born of a woman, under the law, in first-century, Palestinian Judaism. This is God's pattern, the gospel clothed in the culture into which it comes, speaking the language, eating its food, wearing its clothes and learning its customs all the while transforming its citizens by changing their hearts, renewing their minds and restoring their souls. Like salt and light, so is the church, penetrating and illuminating the world of which it is a part. It is fully in the world, but not of it. It is the principle of incarnation. It is God in Christ, the "Word made flesh." It is Christ in the church, the "gospel made flesh" within each culture and people group.[2]

As it grows into the "young adult" stage, a church should be prepared to find its own way of expressing its common faith, loving unity, and sound doctrine. The church has to fit its own culture. Therefore, the church must increasingly multiply local leaders. By appointing elders in every city with prayer and fasting the Apostle Paul empowered the churches to become both self-expressing and self-governing (Acts 14:23). If a church is to multiply it must be able to function with its own resources. It must have its own leaders, and it must support them if it is to be fruitful and multiply in its own culture and country. Continued dependence on foreign workers and money will prevent a national church from becoming strong and multiplying into a movement. Thus, the church must be taught to raise up local leaders and to support itself by local tithes and offerings. Self-government and self-support go hand-in-hand. The offerings Paul collected from the churches from time to time were for the needy, not for the support of local church leaders. He expected the churches to be financially independent and support their own leaders. He taught that "elders who direct the affairs of the church well…whose work is teaching and preaching, are worthy of double honor, for the Scripture says, 'Do not muzzle the ox while it is treading out the grain' for a worker deserves his wages" (1 Timothy 5:17, 18). Local leaders are to be supported locally.[3]

Further, contextualizing a church within its culture also requires that the church become self-propagating, in addition to having become self-expressing, self-governing and self-support-ing. The way in which a church reaches out, witnesses, and evan-gelizes should be culturally sensitive and financially feasible. The means, methods, and materials used should be appropriate and affordable; otherwise the church may become unnecessarily dependent on outside resources and restrict the development of local resources, thus hindering the health and growth of the work. Wise investment in a national church will focus on empowering it in a way that releases, rather than restricts, in much the same way that parents empower and release their newly wed children to establish their own lives and homes.

The empowering process releases a national church to "try its wings" by nurturing and developing healthy homegrown leaders. It releases the church to "stand on its own two feet" by cultivat-ing and using available local resources. A national church must be empowered to find a way to authentically "flesh out" the gospel within its culture and clearly communicate the good news of Christ in a way that is understood and relevant to unbelievers in its region.

Structuring the Church for Expansion

Empowering the church for continuing growth requires the development of functional and appropriate structures that facil-itate and release growth and expansion. Just as our skeletal struc-tures grow with our bodies, facilitating health and growth, so a church must have structural forms that will aid its continued development and growth.

The Early Church had structure from the beginning. Initially the Jerusalem Church regularly met in the temple and from house to house. The twelve apostles gave themselves to prayer and the ministry of the Word as well as to "waiting on tables" in the distribution of food (Acts 6:1, 2). This required organization and structure. However, the increasing number of disciples required an adjustment in structure as well as in the number and type of leaders. Greek-speaking (Hellenistic) Jews "complained against those of the Aramaic-speaking community because their widows were being overlooked in the daily distribution of food." Wisely the Aramaic-speaking apostles asked the disciples themselves to choose seven men from among them who were known to be full of the Spirit and wisdom. Seven were chosen, and the apostles prayed, laid hands on them, and turned over the responsibility of daily food distribution to them. All seven had Greek names and were apparently Greek-speaking Jews (Acts 6:5). Three major structural, organizational adjustments took place: the number of leaders increased from 12 to 19, the type of leaders expanded to include Greek-speaking Jews who were culturally suitable and spiritually capable of serving, and the apostles were released to focus on their primary responsibilities of prayer and the ministry of the Word. The result was that "The word of God spread. The number of disciples in Jerusalem increased rapidly, and a large number of priests became obedient to the faith" (Acts 6:7). The restructuring aided growth and expansion. The wineskin (structure) was flexible, allowing the wine (the body of believers) to grow and expand. Sometime later the structure was again expanded to include leaders who were elders, apparently appointed to oversee the growing ministry of the church in Jerusalem (Acts 11:30; 15:6).[4]

Such release of ministry through restructuring and expanding the number of leaders is but another example of what Moses learned from the counsel of his father-in-law Jethro: "The work is too heavy for you; you cannot handle it alone…select capable men from all the people…and appoint them as officials over thousands, hundreds, fifties and tens [and] have them serve as judges for the people at all times; but have them bring every difficult case to you; the simple cases they can decide themselves. That will make your load lighter, because they will share it with you." Wisely, Moses "listened to his father-in-law and did everything he said," and he was "able to stand the strain." Further, because Moses adjusted the structure, "all the people went home satisfied" (Exodus 18:18-26). Growth and expansion require structure and organization that are flexible and releasing rather than inflexible and restricting.

Structure and organization do not make a church grow, but they can release or restrict life and growth. The Apostle Paul's example of appointing elders in each church is instructive (Acts 14:23), and he told Titus to follow the same practice. "The reason I left you in Crete was that you might set in order the things left unfinished and appoint elders in every town" (Titus 1:5). He then gave clear instructions as to the qualifications of such leaders so that sound (literally, "healthy") doctrine would be taught and believers built up (Titus 1:6-9). He also gave similar instructions to Timothy in Ephesus concerning the appointment of qualified elders who teach, preach and direct the affairs of the church, so that people would know "how to conduct themselves in God's household, which is the church of the living God" (1 Timothy 3:1-15). Now if God's family is the church of the living God, we would expect it to be alive and growing. Such life and growth had to be nourished, and this required the multiplication of "reliable men who will also be qualified to teach others" (2 Timothy 2:2). In addition to establishing guidelines for overseeing elders, Paul also gave instruction about deacons who, after first being tested, were to serve. As in Jerusalem, adequately caring for widows was a necessary ministry in the churches in Ephesus as well.[5]

Facilitating growth and ministry requires structure and organization. The question is not whether or not a church needs structure and organization. The question is what kind and when. Are the structure and organization functional? Do they release or restrict? Are they appropriate and a good fit culturally? As a church grows, developing needed and suitable ministries becomes a high priority. Ministry to families, to children, to youth, to adults, to special groups in need is essential. Releasing such ministries will require structuring the church for expansion, not for mere maintenance in ministry. Such structure needs to be simple and flexible, allowing and supporting growth and expansion. This is especially true as the church not only grows and expands but also multiplies and begins other churches. Multi-church, regional, national, and global structures will become necessary, requiring more leaders as well as different kinds of leaders.[6]

Contextualizing, Unifying, and Nationalizing the Work

As the Foursquare work in Papua New Guinea began to multiply congregations, it became clear that the national church needed to be given its "wings" and allowed to establish its own vision and leadership. Part of the process was the development of a national constitution and bylaws that incorporated what was needed doctrinally and structurally, while fitting into the cultural milieu that surrounded it. In addition, the infrastructure of the national church was developed, multiplying regions, districts, and areas, empowering key leaders to cast vision, develop young leaders, and establish ministry points in their areas. The result was a sense of ownership on the part of the national leadership. This ownership led to a continued rapid development of churches, schools, and medical centers throughout the country. The Foursquare Church in Papua New Guinea now consists of more than 1,000 local congregations and a presence in all 19 provinces. Their goal is to reach the entire nation with the gospel.

Multiplying the Church to Expand: The Sponsoring Process

As the church expands, an outward focus becomes more and more apparent, and fruitfulness moves toward multiplication. Expansion begins as the church reaches its own "Jerusalem," that is, the church reaches people who are of the same or similar culture and live in the same community. Expansion continues as the church reaches people of the same or similar culture who live in the larger region, that is its own "Judea." Such expanding witness increasingly involves collaboration whereby congregations mutually assist one another in outreach. This sponsoring process is accomplished in two ways: by working together to evangelize a community and a region, and by working together to multiply new congregations.

Evangelizing a Community

Jesus promised his disciples that when the Holy Spirit came upon them they would receive power to be his witnesses, starting "in Jerusalem and in all Judea and Samaria and to the ends of the earth" (Acts 1:8). Beginning with the Day of Pentecost, that is exactly what happened as the witness to Christ initially expanded in Jerusalem and Judea. Expanding from 120 disciples in an upper room to 3,000 converts ten days later, the Jerusalem Church saw added to its number day by day those who were being saved (Acts 2:42). In less than two years the number of those who believed grew to 5,000 men, not counting women and children (Acts 4:4). Even after the sudden death of Ananias and Sapphira, "more and more men and women believed and were added to their number" (Acts 5:14). As a result of miraculous healings by the apostles, crowds from towns around Jerusalem took their sick and possessed to be healed. Indeed, Jerusalem was being filled with the apostles' teaching, and the gospel was spreading into the surrounding region (Acts 5:16, 29). And of the thousands who believed, most were Jews. The gospel was reaching those of the same or similar culture in Jerusalem and Judea.

A similar pattern of expanding witness in a community and surrounding region took place in Antioch in Syria (Acts 11:19-26; 13:1-4), in Thessalonica in Greece (Acts 17:1-4; 1 Thessalonians 1:7-10), and in Ephesus in western Turkey (Acts 19:8-20;

Colossians 1:6-8). How did this happen? Was it strategic or spontaneous? Was it planned or unplanned? It probably was both. The expanding witness was planned by the Holy Spirit, but the believers obeyed spontaneously and were led by the Spirit strategically to reach their community and region with the gospel. Given to regular prayer and fasting, the believers were sensitive to the Spirit's directives as they responded and reached those whom the Lord had prepared to receive the gospel.[7] The working together of the Body of Christ "standing firm in one spirit, contending as one man for the faith of the gospel" even under increasing opposition caused the gospel to spread widely and rapidly (Philippians 1:27). The Church was united and the world believed.[8]

Enlarging the vision of a church to see the lost as "sheep without a shepherd" is vital. A church with this kind of a vision can grow into a region-wide movement. Learning to experience the Father's heart for lost sheep is a work of the Spirit of God. It is learning to see what God sees and feel what God feels. As the church experiences the compassion of Jesus, it too will be about the Father's business to seek and to save the lost. As a result of an enlarged vision and heart for the lost, the church intentionally, consistently, and unitedly begins to reach out to the society, giving special attention to groups of people that are needy and open to the gospel. Social networks of relationships and common interests become the "nets," and common language and culture become the "bridges" by which people are brought to Jesus. Using those methods and winning numbers of people to Christ will eventually require starting new churches.

Multiplying Congregations

As a church increases in numbers, expansion growth must eventually move into extension growth, which means starting new congregations. In the earliest days the Church in Jerusalem expanded rapidly and even people from surrounding areas in

Judea came to Jerusalem for ministry. "Crowds gathered...from the towns around Jerusalem, bringing their sick and those tormented by evil spirits, and all of them were healed" (Acts 5:16). But as persecution increased, many believers, especially Hellenistic Jews, were scattered throughout Judea and Samaria. And "those who had been scattered preached the word wherever they went" (Acts 8:4). As a result the Church began to multiply throughout Palestine. Expansion growth now gave way to extension growth as new congregations began to appear. Fruitfulness now began to result in multiplication, and within less than ten years churches were found throughout Judea, Galilee, and Samaria (Acts 9:31). The movement of believers was no longer toward Jerusalem, but from Jerusalem. Jerusalem was no longer the center, as in the Old Testament, where people went to meet God. Rather, Jerusalem became the center from which the gospel spread throughout the region and beyond, with people coming to know the Lord even as far away as Phoenicia in Lebanon, the island of Cyprus and Antioch in Syria (Acts 11:19).

A similar pattern developed in Ephesus in western Turkey. Although Paul stayed in the city ministering in the hall of Tyrannus for two years, the word of God spread throughout the whole region "so that all the Jews and Gentiles who live in the province of Asia heard the word of the Lord" (Acts 19:10). Although large numbers of people came to Christ in Ephesus and the church expanded rapidly, the surrounding region was also touched with the gospel as well. Expansion growth gave way to extension growth as new churches multiplied throughout the province in communities such as Smyrna, Pergamum, Thyatira, Sardis, Philadelphia, Laodicea, and Colosse.

Apparently this pattern of the multiplication of churches characterized the ministry of the Apostle Paul throughout his journeys. How else can his comment be explained when, in less than 25 years after Pentecost, he claimed to have "fully preached the gospel of Christ from Jerusalem all the way around to Illyricum in Albania" (Romans 15:19)? In fact, so thoroughly had the eastern Mediterranean world been penetrated with the gospel, that Paul wanted to move on to Spain lest he "build on someone else's foundation." Of course, much remained to be done to nurture and strengthen the churches that had been planted. Paul and many others had planted, but teachers such as Apollos were needed to water what had been planted so that God could give the growth (1 Corinthians 3:6).

Clearly, incorporating new believers into the family of God resulted in larger congregations and required the starting of more congregations. Although people physically can only grow to a certain size, there is no limit to their growth if they begin to have children, who have children, who have children. Numerical growth becomes exponential; addition becomes multiplication. Such was the case when the Lord told Adam and Eve to "be fruitful and multiply in number...and fill the earth" (Genesis 1:28). After the Flood, God said the same thing to Noah and his sons (Genesis 9:1). If this is true in the physical world, should not the same be true in the spiritual world? Fruitfulness should result in multiplication. How else can the witness of Christ reach the "ends of the earth" (Acts 1:8)? How else can "this gospel of the kingdom be preached in the world as a witness to all nations before the end comes" (Matthew 24:14)?[9]

Evangelizing and Multiplying New Congregations

"Under the leading and power of the Holy Spirit, a handful of foreign missionaries will fan out to some of the central cities of the Philippines, begin evangelistic work, immediately build a strong central church with these converts and open a Bible school where leaders will be trained to go out and pioneer fully indigenous churches in ever expanding circles from the mother church." So wrote Overseas Crusades missions researcher Jim Montgomery about the post World War II growth of The Foursquare Church in the Philippines in his book *New Testament Fire in the Philippines* (p. 187). He reported that The Foursquare Church had grown to nearly 11,000 members in 194 churches and 179 meeting places in 1967. Understanding that the church's work is to preach the gospel and plant congregations in every community, Montgomery observed "everything the Foursquare people do in their churches and much of what they do in their private lives is slanted toward evangelism" (pp. 188-189). Such evangelism and multiplying new congregations has continued to characterize The Foursquare Church in the Philippines, and today there are more than 165,000 members and 4,100 churches and meeting places throughout the nation.

Conclusion

A healthy church multiplies. As it grows up in the Lord and together as a community, it increases numerically and expands. Such fruitfulness prepares the way for exponential growth as it reproduces itself in new congregations. This multiplication process involves empowering the church through helping it to "stand on its own two feet" and structuring it for continued growth. It then begins to expand as it increasingly reaches out and evangelizes its community and region, sponsoring new congregations that in turn sponsor new congregations.

In Stage 3 the planting of new churches through shared resources becomes a lifestyle. Churches are continually trained to sponsor other churches by multiplying and giving away leaders and finances. Strong intercessory prayer becomes vital in strengthening and supporting such church planting as churches and leaders, sensitive to the Holy Spirit, begin multiplying local congregations. When this happens, a church movement becomes a spiritual and strategic tool in the hand of God to reach a region and a nation.

CHAPTER SIX

Disciples of All Nations:
Stage One: Send—Extend

Introduction

The fourth stage builds upon and is the fulfillment of the previous stages. It signals both the climax of a life cycle and the beginning of another life cycle. In this stage the gospel will go full circle, giving rise to and initiating another circle. Like grandparenting, Stage 4 is simultaneously a time of completion and initiation. While one generation is concluding, another is beginning. It is a time when one generation resources and releases another generation. Having freely received the gospel, the national church begins to freely give the gospel as it sends out missionaries both within and beyond its own country. The goal of Stage 4 is to make responsible, reproducing missionary-sending churches. It is the goal of a world-focused national movement that sends and supports both home (national) and foreign (international) missionaries. The task is twofold: networking to reach cultural groups within our region and country and partnering to reach cultural groups in other regions and countries.

Sending to Reach National Cultural Groups: Networking Process

There is a world beyond our own familiar world of what we experience and know. Jesus came to save a world bigger than ours. God so loved the world that He gave His only Son that *whosoever* believes in him should not perish but have everlasting life (John 3:16). God's heart includes all people. He is not willing that any perish, but wants all to come to repentance. The preaching of the gospel of Jesus Christ began in Jerusalem, but it was to go to *all* nations or people groups (*ethne,* Luke 24:47).

Initially Jesus sent his disciples "only to the lost sheep of Israel" (Matthew 10:6). What initially appeared to be a narrow, exclusive, and local commission was actually intended to be a broad, inclusive, and great commission to make disciples of all nations (Matthew 28:20). Both in the Old and New Testament "to the Jew first" was never intended to be "to the Jew only." It was a matter of priority, not prejudice. The blessing of Abraham was not exclusive favoritism but the initiation of blessing designed to reach all the families of the earth through his descendents, the Jews. Upon the death and resurrection of Jesus Christ, his disciples were commissioned to preach repentance and forgiveness of sins in his name to *all* nations. They were to be his witnesses not only to their own Jewish "nation" but also to the Samaritan "nation" and the Gentile "nations" living within and beyond their own land. Those early disciples were to begin where they were, with those living in Jerusalem and Judea who were of similar Jewish background and culture. But then the gospel was to be preached beyond them to the Samaritans who, although also nearby, were of different background and culture. This reaching out would require crossing cultural bridges; it would require what is called "cross-cultural evangelism" or "missions." Reaching other cultural groups is a challenge. It requires increasing world awareness, and it requires sending and supporting missionaries, cross-cultural workers.

Increasing world awareness

A growing awareness of a larger world begins to happen when we have our minds opened to understand what is taught throughout Scripture about Jesus the Messiah, specifically that his suffering, death, and resurrection were for the salvation of *all* nations. This was the mind-opening experience of the two disciples on the road to Emmaus as Jesus "explained to them what was said in all the Scriptures concerning himself" (Luke 24:27). How their hearts burned as he spoke to them and opened the Scriptures. Several hours later, this same mind-opening experience happened to the eleven disciples in Jerusalem when Jesus suddenly appeared behind closed doors and spoke to them. Again, he "opened their minds so they could understand the Scriptures—the messiah will suffer and rise from the dead on the third day *and* repentance and forgiveness of sins will be preached in his name to *all* nations, beginning in Jerusalem" (Luke 24:45-47). What a revelation this was for these Galilean Jews. Jesus is not only the savior of the Jews, He is the Lamb of God that takes away the sin of the world (John 1:29).[1]

In obedience to Christ's instruction to "stay in the city until clothed with power from on high" (Luke 24: 49), the disciples tarried in Jerusalem until they were filled with the Holy Spirit on the Day of Pentecost. Beginning with Peter's message to the gathered throng at Pentecost, the apostles continued to witness boldly about Christ even when they were threatened and imprisoned. Eventually religious opposition and persecution resulted in the death of the first martyr when Stephen, one of the seven appointed deacons, was put to death for his witness to Christ. As a result, a great persecution broke out against the church in Jerusalem and disciples were scattered into non-Jewish territory, preaching the word wherever they went (Acts 8:4).

Thus, the first cross-cultural mission to other people groups was unplanned, more involuntary than voluntary. The witness of Christ had expanded to other "nations" including Samaritans and Gentiles living within and beyond Israel. But this expansion was largely through Hellenistic, bicultural believers such as Philip. The Hebrew apostles and believers apparently were not the focus of the persecution that had broken out, and many, if not most, remained in Jerusalem (Acts 8:1). Apparently it was unbelieving foreign born Hellenistic Jews, such as Saul of Tarsus, who were the driving force behind the persecution (Acts 6:9), and their opposition was directed primarily against Hellenistic Jewish believers. It would appear that the Hebrew Jewish community was largely untouched by the persecution that broke out as a result of the death of a Hellenist believer. However, when the apostles in Jerusalem heard that Samaria had accepted the Word of God through preaching of Philip, they sent Peter and John. When they had prayed for the new believers, the Lord confirmed the inclusion of the Samaritans in the family of faith by giving them the gift of the Holy Spirit as he had the 120 on the Day of Pentecost (Acts 8:14-17). During their return trip to Jerusalem, Peter and John continued the mission to the Samaritans by "preaching the gospel in many Samaritan villages" (Acts 8:25). And later, although it took three visions to prepare a reluctant apostle Peter to go to the house of the Gentile God-fearer Cornelius in Caesarea, he discovered a whitened harvest field as this Roman centurion and his entire household turned to the Lord and received the Spirit as Peter preached the gospel to them (Acts 10).

Within Israel, non-Jewish "nations" were coming to Christ. Home missions was happening. Cross-cultural evangelism was taking place. The apostles were beginning to see what their Scriptures had foretold, that the Messiah would suffer and rise from the dead on the third day and that repentance and forgiveness of sins would be preached in his name to all nations. Disciples were being made of the Samaritan and Gentile nations. Christ's commission to preach the gospel to every creature and to make disciples of all nations was beginning to happen right in their own backyard, within their own country.

Creating world awareness begins with open minds that have come to understand what the Scriptures reveal of God's love for all peoples. From the time of Abraham, God has revealed his purpose to "bless all the families of the earth" (Genesis 12:3).

"The Scripture foresaw that God would justify the Gentiles (nations) by faith and announced the gospel in advance to Abraham: 'All nations will be blessed through you'" (Galatians 3:8). Therefore, "he redeemed us in order that the blessing given to Abraham might come to the Gentiles [nations] through Christ Jesus, so that by faith we might receive the promise of the Spirit" (Galatians 3:14). God's amazing grace is for all.

This growing awareness of a larger world also increases as a church learns to pray. Of all the things the disciples could have asked Jesus to teach them, the one that we know they asked of him was, "Lord, teach us to pray" (Luke 11:1). The "Lord's Prayer" was his response. Of the six requests, the priority is given to God's honor, kingdom, and will. The hallowing of his name by the coming of his kingdom and the doing of his will on earth as it is in heaven is a missionary prayer. Its aim is the honoring of God's name in all the earth. Jesus' primary concern is the glory of the Father throughout all the world. As the gospel of the kingdom is preached in all the world to all nations, more and more people are coming out of the kingdom of darkness into the kingdom of God's Son. This is his will, that none perish but that all come to repentance. It is logical to assume that, as obedient disciples, Jesus' early followers would have learned to pray this way daily. Could it be that behind the Book of Acts is a praying church that, in turn, was taught by the apostles to pray the same way also? When the believers were being persecuted and threatened, their prayer, the longest recorded prayer in Acts, included a quotation from Psalm 2. The believers appealed to God's sovereign purpose in Christ's death and asked him to "enable your servants to speak your word with great boldness (and) stretch out your hand to heal and perform miraculous signs and wonders through the name of your holy servant Jesus" (Acts 4:23-30). The passion of the prayer was for the advance of the gospel and the honoring of God's Son. Further, it is interesting to note that the context of the verses quoted from Psalm 2 is the passage where God says to the Son: "Ask of me and I will make the

nations your inheritance, the ends of the earth your possession"
(Psalm 2:8). This is a missional prayer, echoing the Lord's
Prayer.[2] The Lord heard and answered their prayer, for "after they
prayed the place where they were meeting was shaken and they
were all filled the Holy Spirit and spoke the word of God boldly" (Acts 4:31).

The Early Church was a praying Church. It became "a house
of prayer for all nations" (Mark 11:17). Those early believers
learned to pray for nations; prayer was their highest priority. Paul
urged Timothy that "first of all...requests, prayers, intercession
and thanksgiving be made for everyone—for kings and all those
in authority that we may live peaceful and quiet lives in all god-
liness and holiness. This is good and pleases God our Savior, who
wants all men to be saved and come to a knowledge of the truth"
(1 Timothy 2:1-3).

We must have minds that are open to understand Scripture's
teaching about Christ's death for all and hearts that are open to
intercede for the salvation of all—this increases not only world
awareness but also world involvement. It was to the twelve disciples that Jesus said, "Pray the Lord of the harvest to send out
laborers into his harvest" (Matthew 9:37). And it was those who
so prayed that he sent out (Matthew 10:1-8). It was while the
leaders at the church in Antioch were worshiping and fasting
that the Holy Spirit spoke and said, "Set apart for me Barnabas
and Saul for the work to which I have called them" (Acts 13:2).
After fasting and praying, they laid hands on them and sent
them out. A praying church is a going church.

Sending and supporting missionaries within our country

Missions begins at home. It begins with seeing the shepherdless
multitudes at our doorstep (Matthew 9:35-38). In his first sermon in his hometown of Nazareth, Jesus clearly indicated God's
care for Gentiles. Having quoted Isaiah 61:1, 2, he spoke of the
sending of both Elijah and Elisha to minister to non-Jews: Elijah

to a widow in Sidon, and Elisha to Naaman the Syrian (Luke 4:24-27). Although much of his ministry was to the "lost sheep of Israel," Jesus also preached the good news of the kingdom to "other sheep" as well. From the beginning of his ministry, the news about Jesus spread far beyond Jewish territory. From Syria sick were brought to be healed by him and large crowds from the Decapolis ("ten cities") on the east of the Jordan River followed him (Matthew 4:24, 25). It was in the Gentile region of the Decapolis that Jesus healed a demoniac, instructing him to "return home and tell how much God has done for you" (Luke 8:39). In the region of Tyre and Sidon, Jesus commended the faith of a Canaanite woman, and her faith resulted in the deliverance of her daughter from demons (Matthew 15:21-28). On another occasion Jesus went into the region of the Decapolis and healed a deaf man (Mark 7:31-37). It was while he was on the border between Galilee and Samaria that Jesus healed ten lepers, including a Samaritan, who alone returned to thank him (Luke 16:11-19). And even within Jewish territory, Jesus ministered to a foreigner, healing a Roman centurion's servant in Capernaum (Matthew 8:5-13).

Perhaps the most dramatic story of ministry to an "outsider" is that of the woman at the well in Sychar. Deliberately choosing to go through Samaria rather than taking the usual route east of the Jordan River, Jesus encountered a Samaritan woman. Surprised that he, a Jew, would talk with her a Samaritan, she discovered a man who offered her living water. The result was that she believed and returned to her village, telling her friends about Jesus; many people in that Samaritan village believed because of her testimony. Seeing the response of the Samaritans, Jesus told his amazed disciples, "Do you not say, 'Four months more and then the harvest? I tell you, open your eyes and look at the fields! They are ripe for harvest'" (John 4:35). When the villagers urged Jesus to stay longer, he remained two more days. As Jesus spoke to them, many more became believers declaring, "We no longer believe just because of what you said; now we have heard for ourselves and we know that this man really is the Savior of the world" (John 4:42).

Eventually the way to the "ends of the earth" must go through "Samaria." Some of the greatest barriers to the gospel are not geographic, but cultural and social. Although Pentecost began with the nations gathered in Jerusalem (Acts 2:5-11), it took some time before the Church moved beyond Jewish territory to the nations within their own country. It was the scattering of Hellenistic believers because of persecution that caused the gospel to spread to the Samaritans, people who were geographically near but culturally distant. And even when persecution drove believers into Gentile nations beyond Israel, into such places as Phoenicia, Cyprus, and Antioch in Syria, they initially told the message only to Jews. However, some eventually began to speak to the Gentiles also, "telling them the good news about the Lord Jesus…[for] the Lord's hand was with them, and a great number of people believed and turned to the Lord" (Acts 11:19-21). A bridging of cultural barriers began to take place both within and beyond the nation of Israel. Cross-cultural evangelism was happening both among "the nations" geographically nearby and at a distance.

Today large urban areas have a world of cultures within them. Internal migration and international immigration have resulted in a multicultural population in most large cities. Domestic "home missions" is urgently needed among these "Samaritans" in our communities. They are the foreigners, the immigrants, minorities, and international guests in our cities and in our country. These are the fields ripe for harvest. Workers are needed to take the gospel to them. Missionaries are needed to reach them and establish churches among them.[3] "Doing missions" starts at home, in our communities and in our country. Reaching diverse cultural groups locally and nationally requires churches to network, connecting and cooperating in sending and supporting cross-cultural workers into the whitened fields.

Sending National Missionaries

Josue Bengston was a fruitful evangelist and pastor serving in southern Brazil. The Lord began dealing with his heart about areas of Brazil yet untouched with the gospel, especially in the northern part of the country. In the 1980s Josue, along with his family, was sent as a missionary to the Amazon region in the north. Planting a church in the city of Belem, the capital of the State of Para, Josue began training workers and holding evangelistic meetings. New meeting places were established and new congregations were begun, first in Belem, then in other communities, and eventually along the Amazon as far inland as Manaus. Today more than 300 churches are found in the Amazon region of Brazil. And the work continues to expand into unreached areas along the tributaries of the Amazon River. The Foursquare Church is now evangelizing in every one of the 26 states of the country of Brazil.

Partnering to Reach Distant Cultural Groups

The gospel knows no boundaries because love knows no boundaries. The gospel can grow wherever it is planted, for it is the power of God to save all who believe. God so loved the world that he gave his Son so that whoever believes can have everlasting life. The gospel is international. It must be preached in all the world as a witness to all nations before the end comes when Christ returns. The mandate of our Master calls us to "preach the good news to all creation, to be his witnesses to the ends of the earth and to make disciples of all peoples" (Mark 16:15; Acts 1:8; Matthew 28:20). Clearly the universal proclamation of the gospel calls for both networking within our country and partnering internationally. It requires the sending and supporting of missionaries beyond our national boundaries and the reaching of groups yet unreached with the gospel of Jesus Christ.

Sending and supporting missionaries beyond our country

The Spirit of God is ever speaking of "the regions beyond." Therefore, sensitivity to the Spirit's call and leading is essential. There is a season for sending. While the leaders at the church in Antioch were worshiping and fasting, the Holy Spirit spoke and called Barnabas and Saul to "foreign missions" (Acts 13:2). The church in Antioch was already involved in "home missions," reaching not only Jews but also Greeks (Acts 11:20-26). This was the church that sent offerings to needy Jewish believers in Judea (Acts 11:27-30). This was the church led by an international team of prophets and teachers (Acts 13:1). This was a church with a heart for the world. This was a worshiping, fasting, praying church, a church prepared to hear and heed the Spirit's call and direction. Thus, when the Spirit spoke saying, "Set apart for me Barnabas and Saul for the work to which I have called them," the church responded. When they had fasted and prayed, they commissioned and sent out two of their primary leaders (Acts 13:3). So began the first apostolic missionary journey to "the regions beyond."

Led by the Holy Spirit, Barnabas and Saul (who was also called Paul) went "back home," returning to the lands of their birth, to the island of Cyprus and to central Turkey (Acts 13:4-14:26). Preaching the gospel in the power of the Holy Spirit, Barnabas and Paul led many Jews and Gentiles to the Lord, including the Roman proconsul of Cyprus. Churches planted, believers were taught, and disciples were strengthened and encouraged to remain true to the faith even when persecuted. In every church elders were appointed; with prayer and fasting, believers were "committed to the Lord in whom they had put their trust" (Acts 14:22, 23). Having completed the work to which the Spirit had called them, Barnabas and Saul returned to Antioch and reported to the church "all God had done through them and how he had opened the door of faith to the Gentiles" (Acts 14:27).

The conversion of Gentiles to faith in Christ caused a crisis. Jewish believers from Judea traveled to Antioch and began teaching that Gentiles could not be saved unless they were circumcised and obeyed the Law. Such a sharp dispute arose that Paul and Barnabas, along with other believers, were sent to Jerusalem to see the apostles and elders about this question. The conclusion of this "Jerusalem Council" was that both Gentiles and Jews are saved "through the grace of our Lord Jesus Christ." Peter reminded those gathered of his experience in the house of Cornelius. "God showed he accepted them [Gentiles] by giving the Holy Spirit to them, just as he did to us. He made no distinction between us and them, for he purified their hearts by faith" (Acts 11:25-17; 15:7-11). Quoting the prophet Amos, James pointed out how God demonstrated his concern by taking from the Gentiles a people for himself (Amos 9:11, 12). Therefore, speaking on behalf of the apostles and elders, James concluded, "we should not make it difficult for the Gentiles who are turning to God" (Acts 15:19).[4] Circumcision was not essential to salvation. Circumcision could continue to be practiced by Jews, but Gentiles were not to be compelled to be circumcised, for circumcision is a matter of the heart (Romans 2:28, 29). The result of this decision was momentous. It opened wide the door of faith to the Gentiles because they did not have to become Jews to be Christians. Mission to the Gentiles was now not just "kosher"; it was imperative. And so the church at Antioch continued to send out and support apostolic teams to, in the words of the Apostle Paul, "call people from among all the Gentiles [nations] to the obedience of that comes from faith" in Jesus Christ (Romans 1:5).

A strong and vibrant church such as the church in Antioch will become a missionary-sending church. Called and gifted Ephesians 4:11 ministry is the key. As it did in Antioch, the anointed ministry of apostles, prophets, evangelists, pastors and teachers will equip and prepare the church to be witnesses both in Jerusalem and Judea as well as in Samaria and to the ends of the earth. Sending and supporting workers to the "nations," both within and beyond national boundaries, is how another "life cycle" begins. It is the way that disciples are made in all nations.

Reaching unreached groups

From the time of Abraham, God intended all families, all nations, to be blessed through him. All nations were to know and enjoy the blessings of an eternal covenant relationship with God (Genesis 12:2,3; Galatians 3:8, 14). All nations were to know God. All nations were to be his people. All nations were to know his presence.[5] Therefore, the gospel must be preached to all the families, all the nations of the earth. All must hear of God's salvation through his Son, Jesus Christ.

And so the Apostle Paul's constant passion was to preach the gospel where Christ was not yet known. His desire was based on a clear understanding of the Old Testament. Having "fully proclaimed the gospel of Christ" from Jerusalem all the way around to Illyricum (Albania), he claimed that there was no more place for him to work in those regions lest he would "be building on someone's else's foundation. Rather, as it is written, 'Those who were not told about him will see, and those who have not heard will understand'" (Romans 15:20, 21). Paul quoted Isaiah 52:15, which is the introduction to Isaiah 53. The revelation of God's suffering servant who was "pierced for our transgressions, crushed for our iniquities…and by whose wounds we are healed" (Isaiah 53:5) was not just for the Jewish nation, but for all nations. "The Lord will lay bare his holy arm in the sight of all the nations, and all the ends of the earth will see the salvation of our God" (Isaiah 52:10). Paul knew the he was called to the nations. On his first missionary journey, the apostle, quoting from Isaiah (49:6), explained why he preached the gospel not only to the Jews but also to the Gentiles. This is what the Lord had commissioned him to do: "I have made you a light for the

Gentiles, that you may bring salvation to the ends of the earth" (Acts 13:47). The apostle's heartfelt desire and prayer were not just for the salvation of his fellow countrymen, the Jews, but for the salvation of the nations. "But how can they hear without someone preaching to them? And how can they preach unless they are sent? As it is written, "How beautiful are the feet of those who bring good news!'" (Romans 10:15; Isaiah 52:7).

Paul was a frontier missionary who felt compelled to reach those previously unreached with the gospel. That was why he planned to go to Spain. Thus, when he wrote to the church in Rome, he told them of his plans to visit them on his way to Spain. He anticipated that they would be mutually encouraged by each other's faith, and he invited them "to assist him on his journey" (Romans 15:24). Although Paul had never been to the church in Rome, he urged them to participate in his mission to preach the gospel where Christ was not known. He was eager to preach the gospel both in Rome and in the western part of the Roman Empire; he was not ashamed of the gospel, because "it is the power of God for the salvation of everyone who believes: first for the Jew and then for the Gentile" (Romans 1:16). In his letter to the Romans, Paul clearly explained the gospel he preached to both Jew and Gentile, for in it "a righteousness from God is revealed, a righteousness that is by faith from first to last" (Romans 1:17). Since "all have sinned and come short of the glory of God," all are "justified freely [forgiven and pardoned] by his grace through the redemption that came by Christ Jesus" (Romans 3:23, 24). Because the wages of sin is death, God sent his Son as a sacrifice for sin, laying on him the iniquity of us all. "He was delivered over to death for our sins and was raised to life for our justification" (Romans 4:25). This was the gospel Paul was commissioned to preach to Jews and Gentiles alike. And this is the gospel we who have freely received it are to freely give to all people. This is the gospel that is to be taken "to the ends of the earth" (Acts 1:8). This will require the whole Church to take the whole gospel to the whole world.

The gospel of the kingdom is to be preached in all the world as a witness to all nations before the end comes (Matthew 24:14). The spread of the gospel is both geographical and cultural. It is to be preached "in all the world" (*oikoumene*, "inhabited earth") as a witness "to all nations" (*ethne*, peoples). As we have seen in the Book of Acts the expansion of the gospel was not only geographical but also cultural as it spread from Jerusalem throughout Palestine and beyond, to Phoenicia, Cyprus, and Antioch (Acts 9:31; 11:19). Though the gospel spread widely in terms of geography, the preaching of the gospel tended to spread along cultural lines. Thus, even though Jewish believers traveled as far as Antioch, they spoke "only to Jews" (Acts 11:19). This was monocultural evangelism, since the believers were speaking to people of the same culture. This has been called E-1 evangelism, believers telling the message to their own kind of people no matter what the geographical distance, whether Jerusalem or Antioch. When Jewish believers from Cyprus and Cyrene began to speak to the Greeks (non-Jews), they were engaging in cross-cultural evangelism, which has been called E-2 and E-3 evangelism.[6] They did not just cross the spiritual barrier between believers and unbelievers; they crossed cultural barriers between Jews and Gentiles. Such cross-cultural evangelism is what Jesus did with the Samaritan woman, what Peter did with Cornelius, and what Philip did with the Ethiopian eunuch. All of those cross-cultural evangelism encounters took place within Palestine, a geographically small region. Such cross-cultural evangelism is the kind of evangelism required to reach people who are culturally different. "The ends of the earth" is not simply geographical; it can be cultural. The distance traveled is more a matter of cultural distance than geographical distance. As someone has said, "It is not the number of miles traveled. It is the last eighteen inches that count, the distance between two people of different cultures." Paul was a cross-cultural missionary. Although he went to the Jews first, his primary call was to be an "apostle to the Gentiles." Peter was a monocultural missionary. Although at times he spoke to Gentiles such as Cornelius, his primary call was to be an "apostle to the Jews" (Galatians 2:7, 8). Both preached the gospel "in all the world" geographically, but Paul was a witness to the nations.

Frequently people of a different customs and cultures are either overlooked or bypassed in evangelism. Reaching our own kind of people is easier and less intimidating. Sometimes racial pride and prejudice may be involved. Apparent resistance to the gospel may be a reason some groups are neglected. Seldom is the issue geographical distance. This is why Jesus challenged his disciples to "open their eyes and look at the fields" when they were in Samaria (John 4:35). Even after the Day Pentecost the believers appear to have been rather slow in taking the gospel to the Samaritans. It was quite some time, after Christians were driven out of Jerusalem by persecution, before the good news about Jesus reached Samaria through the preaching of Philip (Acts 8:5-17). The Samaritans were an overlooked and bypassed people group who, when the gospel finally did come to them, were surprisingly receptive, as were the Gentile nations when Paul preached the gospel to them (Acts 13:45-47).[7]

We have seen that disciples are to be made of all nations. They may be nearby nations (*ethne*) or nations (*ethne*) further away. Like the Samarians in Samaria and the Gentiles in Cornelius' house in Caesarea, they may be in the same country. Or they may be further away in another country, like the Jews and Gentiles in Antioch in Syria. All are considered "unreached nations" until the gospel is preached, converts won, believers discipled, and sufficient churches established to create a national movement that can eventually evangelize the entire group.[8] In the first century such national movements took place in Palestine among the Jews and Samaritans, and then spread to Diaspora Jews and the Gentile nations in Syria, Cyprus, Turkey and Greece. The gospel spread to the entire Roman Empire and, over the centuries, to all of Europe and the Americas, eventually reaching around the globe. Disciples are now found in almost every country of the world. Geographically the gospel has become universal. Today the gospel is being preached "in all the world." What remains is the "witness to all nations" within these countries.[9]

Today making "disciples of all nations" continues to take place as strong national church movements develop and missionaries are sent to those yet unreached with the gospel. Such pioneer missionaries are particularly needed among the thousands of cultures located in the countries within what has been called the "10/40 window," the area between 10 and 40 degrees north latitude stretching from the west coast of Africa through the Middle East and central Asia to the Far East and Southeast Asia.[10] Half the world's population lives within this "window." Most are Muslims, Hindus, and Buddhists who have never heard or understood the good news of the gospel. Within every unreached people group or "nation" in these countries, a strong national church movement must be birthed and the gospel preached to all within it and disciples made who become witnesses to the transforming power of the gospel. Therefore, the work of frontier pioneer missions is of highest priority until there is "a witness to *all* nations."

Sending International Missionaries and Reaching Unreached Groups

Nigeria has seen a significant population explosion, going from 16 million people in 1900 to more than 100 million in 2000; the population is projected to double within the next 30 years. With half the population now Christian, Nigeria, once the focus of missions efforts, is now a missionary-sending country. It is estimated that for every missionary sent to Nigeria five are going out as missionaries to other fields, including many unreached groups. The Nigerian Evangelical Missions Association (NEMA) was organized in the early 1980s as an umbrella agency to coordinate and support the missions efforts of more than 100 Nigerian denominations and mission agencies including The Foursquare Church. Their plan is to mobilize 50,000 Nigerians within the next 15 years to take the gospel through all the African countries and the Arabian Peninsula in a "Back to Jerusalem" movement (source: *Global Prayer Digest,* February 8, 2008, p. 13).

Conclusion

Stage 4 is perhaps one of the most challenging stages of all as a church and a national movement bridge into new cultures, moving from mono-cultural evangelism to cross-cultural mission. Bridging into under-evangelized and unreached groups both within its own country and beyond requires networking and partnering with other churches to send and support missionaries. Connecting and collaborating is vitally important in pioneering new frontiers. Of highest priority is intercessory prayer as the church prays to the Lord of the harvest to send forth workers into his harvest. In identifying, preparing, sending and supporting those whom God has called the church truly becomes a co-laborer with Him in His redemptive mission to seek and save the lost from every tongue, tribe, kindred, and nation.

Disciples of All Nations...
Until He Comes

Christ's commission to make disciples of all nations is possible, for with the mandate comes the promise of his presence, power, and authority. He will be with us to the end of the age. His Spirit has empowered us to be his witnesses to the ends of the earth. He has sent us with his authority, the authority of the One who has all authority in heaven and on earth. Yes, it is "mission possible," for faithful is the One who has called us; he will do it—through his Church, through us.

Today the gospel of the kingdom is being preached in the whole world. The witness to all nations is increasing. Today we are closer than ever before to fulfilling Christ's mandate. It can be done! It must be done, done as the first century church did it—by developing a reproducible life cycle that continually extends the gospel into every unreached group until disciples are made in *every* nation. We know that this mission will be completed, for John saw a "great multitude no one could count...before the throne and in front of the Lamb" and they were from "*every* nation, tribe, people and language "(Revelation 7:9). All peoples are present, the "register of the peoples" is complete (Psalm 87:6, 7).

When will the Great Commission be completed? When can it be said, "It is finished"? When He comes! Until then we are to be about the Father's business, for His will is that none perish, but all come to repentance. Surely the Lamb is worthy to receive the reward of His suffering, for with His blood He "purchased men for God from *every* tribe, and language, and people and nation" (Revelation 5:9). The price has been paid. Disciples must be made, for "He died for all, that those who live should no longer live for themselves but for him who died and was raised again" (2 Corinthians 5:15). "God's goal is that His Son's name be exalted and honored among all the peoples of the world."[1] This is our goal. For this reason the International Church of the Foursquare Gospel is "dedicated unto the cause of inter- denominational and world wide evangelism," dedicated to the making of disciples of all nations...until He comes.

National Church Development:
A Local Assessment

Instructions:

Please assign a numeral from 1 (not happening) to 10 (continually happening) to each statement as it applies to your church. Write the numeral in the space next to each statement. Add the four numerals in each category, and record the total. Divide this total by four, and record the average for the category. Do this with each of the sixteen categories.

Stage 1: Initiate—evangelizing. Goal: to make responsible, reproducing disciples

A. Birthing process (communicating the gospel)

1. Finding the lost
____ a. Evangelism is a high priority in our church.
____ b. Our church is outward focused and involved in ministry in our community
____ c. Our people befriend and show love to unbelievers.
____ d. Our church reaches out to the lost and seeks to share the gospel with them.

Total: ____ divide by 4 =____ (average)

2. Winning the lost

____ a. Our church is evangelistic and wins the lost to Christ.

____ b. Each year we see a larger number of people coming to Christ.

____ c. Personal relationships with believers is a major reason unbelievers come to Christ through our church.

____ d. Our church tries to find and use evangelistic methods that work.

Total: ____ *divide by 4 =* ____ *(average)*

B. Bonding process (planting the church)

3. Incorporating believers

____ a. The church does follow-up with new converts.

____ b. Each year more of our new converts are being baptized in water.

____ c. New converts are welcomed and made to feel at home in our church.

____ d. New converts are becoming active members in our church.

Total: ____ *divide by 4 =* ____ *(average)*

4. Discipling believers

____ a. New believers are taught and trained to continue to follow the Lord.

____ b. People are baptized and filled with the Holy Spirit.

____ c. People are taught to regularly spend time in prayer and God's word.

____ d. People are taught to reach out with the gospel to their family and friends.

Total: ____ *divide by 4 =* ____ *(average)*

Stage 2: Nurture—strengthening. Goal: to make responsible, reproducing leaders

A. Modeling process (developing godly character)

5. Strengthening family life

___ a. The marriages of the people who attend our church are getting stronger.

___ b. Families are taught to develop loving and caring relationships in the home.

___ c. Parents are taught how to raise godly children.

___ d. Children are being brought to Christ and follow the Lord.

Total: ____ divide by 4 = ____ (average)

6. Cultivating congregational life

___ a. There is a spirit of love and acceptance.

___ b. People become friends and enjoy fellowship with one another.

___ c. People worship freely and express their love for the Lord openly.

___ d. There is a sense of the presence of the Lord in our church.

Total: ____ divide by 4 = ____ (average)

B. Mentoring process (releasing ministry)

7. Mobilizing members

____ a. Members are taught their place in the Body of Christ and equipped to use their divinely given abilities/gifts to serve others.

____ b. People are taught to tithe and give faithfully.

____ c. People volunteer to help when needs arise.

____ d. There is a spirit of teamwork in our church.

Total: ____ *divide by 4 =* ____ *(average)*

8. Developing leaders

____ a. Training and releasing leaders are high priorities.

____ b. Parents, especially fathers, are learning how to lead their families well.

____ c. The pastors and leaders in our church train others to do what they do.

____ d. Most leaders are raised up from within our congregation.

Total: ____ *divide by 4 =* ____ *(average)*

Stage 3: Expand—multiplying. Goal: to make responsible, reproducing congregations

A. Empowering process (releasing the church)

9. Contextualizing the church

_____ a. Our church develops ways of doing ministry that meet people's needs.

_____ b. The worship, preaching, and teaching fit our culture and the gospel does not look "foreign."

_____ c. Our church is self-supporting and not dependent on outside funds.

_____ d. People in our church live lives that make the gospel attractive and help draw unbelievers to Christ.

Total: _____ divide by 4 = _____ (average)

10. Structuring the church

_____ a. Our church is organized in a way that promotes continuous spiritual growth and maturity in every age group.

_____ b. Our church is structured so that younger leaders can be developed and released into leadership.

_____ c. We find ways to facilitate and network with Bible institutes/schools for training those who are called into full-time Christian ministry.

_____ d. Our bylaws and structure ensure sound doctrine, while making room for numerical growth and multiplication.

Total: _____ divide by 4 = _____ (average)

B. Sponsoring process (multiplying into a movement)

Evangelizing the community

____ a. Evangelism is more of a way of life in our church than a periodic emphasis.

____ b. Members are encouraged to show the love of God in practical ways by meeting the needs of people in the community.

____ c. Both new and older believers are learning how to win their families and friends to Christ.

____ d. More people are coming into our church as a result of being won to Christ than as a result of transferring from other Christian churches.

Total: ____ divide by 4 = ____ (average)

12. Multiplying new congregations

____ a. Our church creates an atmosphere of faith and vision for starting new churches.

____ b. Our church trains leaders to start new churches.

____ c. We start churches that, in turn, start more new churches.

____ d. Our church has a clear plan to plant, support, and nurture new churches throughout our area, especially where people are largely unevangelized.

Total: ____ divide by 4 = ____ (average)

Stage 4: Send—extending. Goal: to make responsible, reproducing missionary-sending churches

A. Networking process (reaching nearby cultural groups)

13. Increasing world awareness and intercession

____ a. Our church is developing a vision for a world bigger than our own community.

____ b. Our church is learning how to pray and intercede for people of different cultures and countries.

____ c. Our church is reaching out and showing the love of God to people of different cultures in our community.

____ d. Our constituency includes people of different cultures that are found in our community.

Total: ____ divide by 4 = ____ (average)

14. Sending and supporting missionaries within our nation

____ a. Our church encourages a "home missions" vision for reaching out to immigrants and minority groups in our community or region.

____ b. We have a clear plan to plant, support and nurture new churches in large urban areas to reach different cultural groups within them.

____ c. Our church sends and supports teams that reach immigrants and minority groups in large urban areas.

____ d. Our church sends and supports missionaries that reach different cultural groups within large urban areas.

Total: ____ divide by 4 = ____ (average)

B. Partnering process (reaching distant cultural groups)

15. Sending and supporting missionaries beyond our nation

____ a. Our church is developing a vision for "world missions."

____ b. Our church faithfully prays and gives to help advance of the gospel through Foursquare missionaries and churches in other countries.

____ c. Our church encourages young people and releases experienced leaders to serve short term or long term in other countries.

____ d. Our church partners with other Foursquare churches to open and develop new fields and raise up national churches in other countries.

Total: ____ *divide by 4 =* ____ *(average)*

16. Bridging into unreached groups

____ a. Our church understands and has a vision for reaching groups of people who are currently beyond the reach of the gospel.

____ b. Our church prays for and supports efforts to reach unreached groups of people in our own country.

____ c. Our church prays for and supports efforts to reach unreached people groups in other countries, especially in the "10/40 window."

____ d. Our church partners with Foursquare churches in other countries to reach unreached groups, continuing efforts until there is a strong national church planting movement in every unreached group.

Total: ____ *divide by 4 =* ____ *(average)*

Summary and Analysis:

1. Place a dot on the appropriate "line" within "the wheel" below based on the average score for each of the sixteen categories with the "hub" representing a score of 1 and the "rim" a score of 10. Join the dots to see how balanced the "wheel" is for your church.

2. Total the four averages in each of the four stages and record them here:
   Stage 1 _____ Stage 2 _____ Stage 3 _____ Stage 4 _____
   In what stages are you strongest? Weakest? Why?

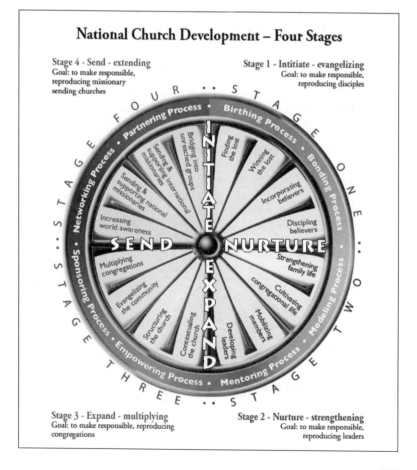

National Church Development – Four Stages

Stage 4 - Send - extending
Goal: to make responsible, reproducing missionary sending churches

Stage 1 - Intitiate - evangelizing
Goal: to make responsible, reproducing disciples

Stage 3 - Expand - multiplying
Goal: to make responsible, reproducing congregations

Stage 2 - Nurture - strengthening
Goal: to make responsible, reproducing leaders

3. Select the response below that best describes your present attitude as a church toward change:

    a.   No change is needed. We are OK the way we are.

    b.   Change is needed. Who will do it for us?

    c.   Change is needed. What are other organizations like ours doing?

    d.   Change is needed. Help us; we want to learn.

    e.   We want to change and are willing to pay the price.

National Church Development:
A National Assessment

Instructions:

Please assign a numeral from 1 (not happening) to 10 (continually happening) to each statement as it applies to the churches in your country. Write the numeral in the space next to each statement. Add the four numerals in each category, and record the total. Divide this total by four, and record the average for the category. Do this with each of the sixteen categories.

Stage 1: Initiate—evangelizing. Goal: to make responsible, reproducing disciples

A. Birthing process (communicating the gospel)

I. Finding the lost
    ____ a. Evangelism is a high priority in our churches.
    ____ b. Our churches are outward focused and involved in ministry in our communities.
    ____ c. Our people befriend and show love to unbelievers.
    ____ d. Our churches reach out to the lost and seek to share the gospel with them.

Total: ____ *divide by 4 =*____ *(average)*

2. **Winning the lost**
   ___ a. Our churches are evangelistic and win the lost to Christ.
   ___ b. Each year we see a larger number of people coming to Christ.
   ___ c. Personal relationships with believers is a major reason unbelievers come to Christ through our churches.
   ___ d. Our churches try to find and use evangelistic methods that work.

   Total: ___ *divide by 4 =* ___ *(average)*

B. Bonding process (planting the church)

3. **Incorporating believers**
   ___ a. The churches do follow-up with new converts.
   ___ b. Each year more of our new converts are being baptized in water.
   ___ c. New converts are welcomed and made to feel at home in our churches.
   ___ d. New converts are becoming active members in local churches.

   Total: ___ *divide by 4 =* ___ *(average)*

4. **Discipling believers**
   ___ a. New believers are taught and trained to continue to follow the Lord.
   ___ b. People are baptized and filled with the Holy Spirit.
   ___ c. People are taught to regularly spend time in prayer and God's word.
   ___ d. People are taught to reach out with the gospel to their family and friends.

   Total: ___ *divide by 4 =* ___ *(average)*

Stage 2: Nurture—strengthening. Goal: to make responsible, reproducing leaders

A. Modeling process (developing godly character)

5. Strengthening family life

____ a. The marriages of the people who attend our churches are getting stronger.

____ b. Families are taught to develop loving and caring relationships in the home.

____ c. Parents are taught how to raise godly children.

____ d. Children are being brought to Christ and follow the Lord.

Total: ____ divide by 4 = ____ (average)

6. Cultivating congregational life

____ a. There is a spirit of love and acceptance in our churches.

____ b. People become friends and enjoy fellowship with one another.

____ c. People worship freely and express their love for the Lord openly.

____ d. There is a sense of the presence of the Lord in our churches.

Total: ____ divide by 4 = ____ (average)

B. Mentoring process (releasing ministry)

7. Mobilizing members

_____ a. Members are taught their place in the Body of Christ and equipped to use their divinely given abilities/gifts to serve others.

_____ b. People are taught to tithe and give faithfully.

_____ c. People volunteer to help when needs arise.

_____ d. There is a spirit of teamwork in our churches.

Total: _____ *divide by 4 =* _____ *(average)*

8. Developing leaders

_____ a. Training and releasing leaders are high priorities.

_____ b. Parents, especially fathers, are learning how to lead their families well.

_____ c. The pastors and leaders in our churches train others to do what they do.

_____ d. Most leaders are raised up from within the local congregations.

Total: _____ *divide by 4 =* _____ *(average)*

Stage 3: Expand—multiplying. Goal: to make responsible, reproducing congregations

A. Empowering process (releasing the church)

9. Contextualizing the church

___ a. Our churches develop ways of doing ministry that meet people's needs.

___ b. The worship, preaching, and teaching fit our culture and the gospel does not look "foreign."

___ c. Our churches are self-supporting and not dependent on outside funds.

___ d. People in our churches live lives that make the gospel attractive and help draw unbelievers to Christ.

Total: ___ divide by 4 = ___ (average)

10. Structuring the church

___ a. Our churches are organized in ways that promote continuous spiritual growth and maturity in every age group.

___ b. Our churches are structured so that younger leaders can be developed and released into leadership.

___ c. We find ways to facilitate and network with Bible institutes/schools for training those who are called into full-time Christian ministry.

___ d. Our national and local bylaws and structures ensure sound doctrine, while making room for numerical growth and multiplication.

Total: ___ divide by 4 = ___ (average)

B. Sponsoring process (multiplying into a movement)

11. Evangelizing the community

____ a. Evangelism is more of a way of life in our churches than a periodic emphasis.

____ b. Members are encouraged to show the love of God in practical ways by meeting the needs of people in their communities.

____ c. Both new and older believers are learning how to win their families and friends to Christ.

____ d. More people are coming into our churches as a result of being won to Christ than as a result of transferring from other Christian churches.

Total: ____ *divide by 4 =* ____ *(average)*

12. Multiplying new congregations

____ a. Our churches create an atmosphere of faith and vision for starting new churches.

____ b. Our churches train leaders to start new churches.

____ c. We start churches that, in turn, start more new churches.

____ d. Our churches have a clear plan to plant, support, and nurture new churches throughout our country, especially where people are largely unevangelized.

Total: ____ *divide by 4 =* ____ *(average)*

Stage 4: Send—extending. *Goal: to make responsible, reproducing missionary-sending churches*

A. Networking process (reaching nearby cultural groups)

13. Increasing world awareness and intercession

____ a. Our churches are developing a vision for a world bigger than our own country.

____ b. Our churches are learning how to pray and intercede for people of different cultures and countries.

____ c. Our churches are reaching out and showing the love of God to people of different cultures in our community.

____ d. Our local church constituencies include people of different cultures that are found in their communities.

Total: ____ divide by 4 = ____ (average)

14. Sending and supporting missionaries within our nation

____ a. Our churches encourage a "home missions" vision for reaching out to immigrants and minority groups in their communities.

____ b. Nationally, we have a clear plan to plant, support, and nurture new churches in large urban areas that can reach various cultural groups.

____ c. Our urban churches develop teams to reach immigrants and minority groups in large urban areas.

____ d. Our churches send and support missionaries that reach different cultural groups.

Total: ____ divide by 4 = ____ (average)

B. Partnering process (reaching distant cultural groups)

15. Sending and supporting missionaries beyond our nation

___ a. Our churches are developing a vision for "world missions."

___ b. Our churches faithfully pray and give to help advance of the gospel through Foursquare missionaries and churches in other countries.

___ c. Our churches encourage young people and release experienced leaders to serve short term or long term in other countries.

___ d. Our churches partner with other Foursquare churches to open and develop new fields and raise up national churches in other countries.

Total: ___ *divide by 4 =* ___ *(average)*

16. Bridging into unreached groups

___ a. Our churches understand and have a vision for reaching groups of people who are currently beyond the reach of the gospel.

___ b. Our churches pray for and support efforts to reach unreached groups of people in our own country.

___ c. Our churches pray for and support efforts to reach unreached people groups in other countries, especially in the "10/40 window."

___ d. Our churches partner with Foursquare churches in other countries to reach unreached groups, continuing efforts until there is a strong national church planting movement in every unreached group.

Total: ___ *divide by 4 =* ___ *(average)*

Summary and Analysis:

1. Place a dot on the appropriate "line" within "the wheel" below based on the average score for each of the sixteen categories with the "hub" representing a score of 1 and the "rim" a score of 10. Join the dots to see how balanced the "wheel" is for the churches in your country.

2. Total the four averages in each of the four stages and record them here:

Stage 1 _____ Stage 2 _____ Stage 3 _____ Stage 4 _____

In what stages are you strongest? Weakest? Why?

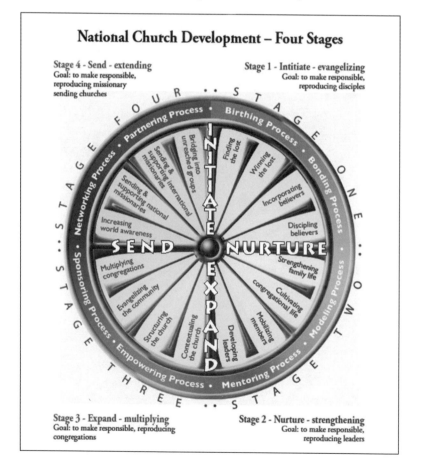

3. Select the response below that best describes your present attitude as a national church toward change:

   a. No change is needed. We are OK the way we are.

   b. Change is needed. Who will do it for us?

   c. Change is needed. What are other organizations like ours doing?

   d. Change is needed. Help us; we want to learn.

   e. We want to change and are willing to pay the price.

Notes

Preface

1. David B. Barrett, George T. Kurian and Todd M. Johnson, *World Christian Encyclopedia*, second edition, volume 1 ,New York: Oxford University Press, 200, p. 3.
2. *World Christian Encyclopedia*, second edition, volume 1, p. 19. Barrett identifies 3 waves of renewal (Pentecostal, charismatic, neo-charismatic) numbering over 500 million members found in 740 Pentecostal denominations, 6530 non-Pentecostal mainline denominations with large organized internal charismatic movements and 18,810 independent neo-charismatics denominations and networks (p. 19).
3. Statistics are from the annual Ministry Report of the International Church of the Foursquare Gospel.
4. Inscribed on the primary cornerstone of Angelus Temple in Los Angeles, California, the first Foursquare church.

Introduction

1. Tim Dowley, editor, *Eerdmans' Handbook to the History of Christianity* (Grand Rapids, MI: Eerdmans, 1977), pp. 66-67. "By the middle of the second century, little more than a hundred years after the death and resurrection of Jesus, flourishing churches existed in nearly all the provinces between Syria and Rome...A century later a significant minority existed in almost every province of the Empire and also in several countries to the east" (p. 65).
2. Roland, Allen, *Missionary Methods: St. Paul's or Ours?* (Grand Rapids, MI: Eerdmans, 1967 reprint), pp. 10-17. See also Wesley D. Balda, editor, *Heirs of the Same Promise: Using Acts as a Study Guide for Evangelizing Ethnic America* (Monrovia, CA: MARC, 1984). "The Book of Acts is about urban evangelization of ethnic peoples and little else" (p. 12).
3. Charles Van Engen, *God's Missionary People: Rethinking the Purpose of the Local Church* (Grand Rapids, MI: Baker, 1993), pp. 43-44. Van Engen identifies seven stages in the emerging of a local and national missionary church which he indicates are repeated time and again in church planting situations. These seven developmental stages are similar in sequence and content to the four stage, 360 degree developmental process proposed by C. Peter Wagner in *Stop the World I Want to Get On* (Ventura, CA: Regal Books, 1973), pp. 103-105 and *On the Crest of the Wave* (Ventura, CA: Regal Books, 1983), pp. 164-165. Foursquare missions has sought to define its strategy in terms of the four-stage developmental process. See Phil Starr,

"What Does It Mean to be a Church Planting Mission?," *Foursquare World Advance* 22 (September/October 1986), p. 5 and Foursquare Missions International's *Global Resource Guide* (1994), pp. 1-2.

Chapter One

1. See "Articles of Incorporation and Bylaws of the International Church of the Foursquare Gospel," (1993 edition), inside front cover.
2. McPherson, Aimee Semple, "Lost and Restored," *This is That* (Los Angeles, CA: Bridal Call Publishing House, 1921), pp. 487-511.
3. The two most comprehensive sources on Foursquare missions are Yeol Soo Eim, "The Worldwide Expansion of the Foursquare Church" (unpublished Doctor of Missiology dissertation, Fuller Theological Seminary, 1986) and Nathaniel M. Van Cleave, *The Vine and the Branches: a History of the International Church of the Foursquare Gospel* (Los Angeles, CA: International Church of the Foursquare Gospel, 1992).
4. Arthur Edwards, "Fishing in Panama," *Foursquare Magazine* (June, 1945), p. 20. See Leland Edwards, *Chasing the Vision* (Lake Mary, FL: Creation House/Foursquare Media, 2006) for a fascinating eyewitness account of the birth and growth of the Foursquare Church in Panama by the son of Arthur Edwards. He writes, "Their vision was for the whole country. The Acts of the Apostles was their 'Manual of Operation'" (p. 28).
5. In both countries the initial focus was on rural tribal groups rather than on urban population centers. As a result the penetration of the country was limited. Lest the impression be given that urban church planting alone is the key to everything, see L. Grant McClung, Jr., "Pentecostal/Charismatic Perspectives on a Missiology for the Twenty-First Century," *Pneuma* 16 (Spring, 1994), pp. 11-22.
6. Jim Montgomery, *New Testament Fire in the Philippines* (Manila, Philippines: C-GRIP, 1972). Foursquare's vision and strategy for the widespread planting of churches throughout the Philippines helped plant a seed in Montgomery's heart. This seed eventually gave birth to the DAWN (Discipling A Whole Nation) movement that seeks to network evangelical and Pentecostal groups to penetrate an entire country with the gospel through saturation church planting. See Jim Montgomery, *Dawn 2000: 7 Million Churches to Go* (Pasadena, CA: Wm. Carey Library, 1989).

Chapter Two

1. An application of the four-stage developmental process to the church in the United States is beginning to take place. See Ray Wheeler, "Church from Another Perspective: Rearranging Assumptions about the Identity

and Work of the Church through an Encounter with World Mission," *Understanding the Times: Key Issues for the Local Church in the 21st Century*, edited by Daniel Brown and Ralph Moore (Kaneohe, HI: Straight Street Publications, 1994), pp. 193-222.

2.   C. Peter Wagner, *Church Planting for a Greater Harvest: a Comprehensive Guide* (Ventura, CA: Regal Books, 1990), pp. 59-75. Based on research Wagner begins his book with this statement: "The single most effective evangelistic methodology under heaven is planting new churches" (p. 11).

3.   See Lawrence E. Keyes, *The Last Age of Missions: a Study of Third World Mission Societies* (Pasadena, CA: Wm. Carey Library, 1983) and Larry D. Pate, *From Every People: a Handbook of Two-Thirds World Missions* (Monrovia, CA: MARC, 1989).

4.   Elsewhere this writer has sought to show how this "full circle" developmental strategy is a key in helping Foursquare make the most of its limited resources. See John L. Amstutz, "Foursquare Missions: Doing More With Less," *Pneuma* (Spring, 1994), pp. 63-80.

Chapter Three

1.   See Acts 10:1-47; 16:13-15, 25-34;18:7, 8 and Acts 6:7; 17:4, 12.

2.   How do people come to Christ? Donald McGavran pointed out that socioeconomic networks and ethnic-linguistic groupings are the primary "bridges of God" to Christ. He called them "people movements." He further stated, "Peoples become Christian fastest when least change of race or clan is involved. When it is felt that 'we are moving with our people and those who have not come now will come later,' then the Church grows most vigorously" (Donald McGavran, *The Bridges of God: a Study in the Strategy of Missions*, Friendship Press, New York, 1955.)

3.   "Poor" is more than economic and social, it is ethical and spiritual. The "poor" are those who are "poor in spirit", who humbly recognize their need of God. They do not look to political schemes, social status or material prosperity for their deliverance and redemption, but to God. It is Jesus himself who embodies the biblical ideal of 'the poor man' who trusts only in God, and herein is the true significance of his poverty, who "though he was rich, yet for your sakes became poor, that you through his poverty might become rich" (2 Corinthians 8:9). See Alan Richardson, *A Theological Word Book of the Bible*, pp. 168-169.

4.   Although perhaps more useful in some cultures than others, James Engel of Wheaton College developed a linear scale showing how people come to Christ through a process of awareness, understanding and personal application of the Gospel and a decision to act (see C. Peter Wagner, *Strategies for Church Growth*, Regal Books, 1987, p. 124).

5. See Acts 8:12-17 (Samaritans), Acts 9:17-19 (Saul of Tarsus), Acts 10:44-47 (household of Cornelius) and Acts 19:1-7 (Ephesians). The reception of the Spirit apparently can take place any time after repentance and faith in Christ. With Cornelius it occurred before water baptism, with the Samaritans and Ephesians after water baptism. However, in every case the Spirit's coming was closely related to water baptism.

6. Matthew 7:28; 11:1; 13:53; 19:1; 26:1. Some have suggested these five sections are a counterpart to the five books of Moses, suggesting Jesus' teaching was to be understood as the fulfillment of the Law (see Matthew 5:17, 18).

7. Genuine happiness (the Beatitudes), transforming witness (salt and light), true righteousness(fulfilling, not merely keeping the law), genuine piety (proper fasting, prayer, almsgiving), singleness of devotion (God or mammon), proper priority (seek first the kingdom of God), non-judgmental discernment (judge not), treating others as you would be treated (golden rule), the broad and narrow way (two gates, paths and destinies), discerning false prophets (by their fruit you know them) and hearing and doing (building upon the rock or sand). John Piper has summarized "all Jesus commanded" as recorded in the four Gospels in fifty demands in his book *What Jesus Demands from the World* (Wheaton IL: Crossway Books, 2006).

8. Baptism "in the Name of Jesus Christ" or "Lord Jesus" in Acts (2:38; 8:16; 10:48; 19:5) is another way of saying "in the Name of the Father, Son and Holy Spirit" since "God was pleased to have all his fullness dwell in him...for in Christ all the fullness of the deity lives in bodily form" (Colossians 1:19; 2:9).

Chapter Four

1. God speaks strongly against "breaking faith...with the wife of your marriage covenant...because he is seeking godly offspring" (Malachi 2:14, 15). In Scripture divorce is permitted for sexual unfaithfulness (*porneia*, Matthew 19:9) and desertion (*chorizo*, 1 Corinthians 7:15) and in such cases, by implication, remarriage is also permitted by the non-offending spouse. Where divorce has taken place, for whatever reason, the raising of godly children by a single parent is a great challenge. And if there has been a remarriage, the same is true for step-parents. In such cases, as with widows and orphans (Psalm 68:5, 6; James 1:27), the church has an increased responsibility and opportunity to "be family" and support such members of the Body of Christ. Healing and helping broken families into greater health and wholeness is one of the increasing challenges the Church faces today. A healthy, loving community of believers is God's

way of helping the hurting. Of the many resources available, one of the more extensive and helpful resources is the ministry of Focus on the Family (www.family.org).

2. The Early Church gathered both in larger and smaller groups both in Jerusalem and beyond (Acts 2:46; 5:42; 19:9, 10; 20:20). Spiritual growth and witness was aided and released by functional and flexible structures. "The large gatherings helped the Church to *grow out* by means of the dynamic impact of their witness of oneness in worship and koinonia while the smaller gatherings helped the Church *grow up* by means of the life-changing impact of ongoing, responsible and personal relationships" (John L. Amstutz, "Beyond Pentecost: A Study of Some Sociological Dimensions of New Testament Church Growth From the Book of Acts," *Essays on Apostolic Themes*, Paul Elbert, editor, Peabody, MA: Hendrikson Publishers, 1985, p. 212). Due to increasing religious, and eventually political, opposition and persecution believers met increasingly in homes (Acts 18:6-8; Romans 16:3-5) as is the case today in countries where the preaching of the gospel and the gathering of believers is not permitted.

3. Some have felt the sharing in the Jerusalem Church was a misguided experiment in economic koinonia and naive generosity, a kind of "Christian communism." However, probably much closer to the truth is the observation of Ron Sider: "Given the hard economic realities in Jerusalem during that time of the first century, it was probably precisely the unusually large number of poor in their midst that made dramatic sharing such an obvious necessity. That the rich among them gave with overflowing generosity to meet a desperate need in the body of Christ indicates not naïve idealism but unconditional discipleship...they dared to give concrete, visible expression to the oneness of believers. In the new messianic community of Jesus' first followers after Pentecost, God was redeeming all relationships" (Ron Sider, *Rich Christians in an Age of Hunger*, Downers Grove, IL: InterVarsity Press, 1977, p. 103).

4. James 4:16; Colossians 3:13; Romans 15:14; Galatians 5:13; Hebrews 10:24; Ephesians 5:21; Ephesians 18, 19; I Peter 1:22. There are over fifty times the phrase "one another" appears in the New Testament epistles alone (see Gene A. Getz, *Sharpening the Focus of the Church*, Chicago, IL: Moody Press, 1974, pp. 155-16).

5. Included are the gifts listed in Romans 12:6-8 and 1 Corinthians 12:7-11, 28. Paul's listing of gifts in Ephesians, Romans and I Corinthians and appears to be suggestive, not exhaustive, since there is overlap and a variety of descriptions of gifts as persons, ministries and manifestations. Peter's description in 1 Peter 4:9, 10 also appears suggestive. C. Peter Wagner's book, *Your Spiritual Gifts Can Help Your Church Grow*, and his spiritual gifts inventory, *Finding Your Spirit Gifts*, is one example of the

many resources available (www.regalbooks.com) in helping understand and identify the spiritual gifts God gives for the building up of the Body of Christ.

6. The words elder/older (*presbuteros*) overseer/bishop (*episcopas*) and shepherd/pastor (*poimenos*) are used interchangeably in the New Testament. See Acts 20: 17, 28 and 1 Peter 5:1-5 and compare 1 Timothy 3:2 with Titus 1:6. Deacon/server (*diakonos*) is used of those who serve. It is used of domestic servants (John 2:5, 9), civil rulers (Romans 13:4; followers of Christ (John 12:26; Ephesians 6:21) and of Christ himself (Romans 15:8; Galatians 2:17). Qualifications for deacons are similar to those of elders (1 Timothy 3:8-13). The focus of these descriptions is more functional than formal, having to do with ministry rather than position. Although the qualifications of elders and deacons are addressed to men, women are not ruled out. Phoebe is described as "being a deaconess" (*diakonon*) in Romans 16:1, Priscilla may well have been a house church pastor (Romans 16:3, 4; Acts 18:24-27) and Junias is identified as being "notable among the apostles" (*apostolois*, Romans 16:7). For a discussion of these biblical examples, including the problematic passages in Paul's letters (1 Corinthians 11:2-16; 14:33-36; 1 Timothy 2:8-15), see *Women in Leadership Ministry* which is "a summary of the biblical position of the Foursquare Church concerning God's grace and a woman's potential under his sovereignty and call" (Foursquare Media, 2007).

7. Comparing 1 Timothy 3:1-7 and Titus 1:5-8 there appear to be at least twenty distinct qualities of an elder/overseer (see Gene Getz, *The Measure of a Man*, Ventura, CA: Regal Books, 1974).

Chapter Five

1. The well-known statement, "In essentials unity, in non-essentials liberty, and in all things charity" expresses the spirit of evangelical Christian groups, including the Foursquare Church. Perhaps one of the most clear and comprehensive contemporary expressions of the essentials of Christian faith is the *Lausanne Covenant* which was produced out of the 1974 International Congress on World Evangelism held in Lausanne, Switzerland, which brought together over 2300 evangelical leaders from 150 countries. Since this initial Lausanne Congress the *Lausanne Covenant* has challenged Christians to work together to make Jesus Christ known throughout the world. Many organizations use this Covenant as their ministry Statement of Faith. A companion document to the *Lausanne Covenant* is the *Manila Manifesto* produced out of the 1989 Lausanne II Congress in Manila, Philippines attended by 4300 evangelical leaders from 173 countries. Affirming the Lausanne

Covenant in "Twenty-One Affirmations", the *Manila Manifesto* clearly explains the meaning of the Lausanne Movement's theme of "The whole Church taking the whole gospel to the whole world." See the Lausanne Committee for World Evangelization website (www.lausanne.org) for a history of the movement and the documents produced of which there are nearly thirty *Lausanne Occasional Papers* (LOP) explaining the essentials of Christian faith and practice.

2. Some have identified these two extremes of under-contextualization and under-contextualization as two types of syncretism. Under-contextualization is "low-end syncretism" where there is not enough engagement with the receiving culture. Thus the church can develop an unhealthy reluctance to give up foreign ways of expressing the gospel and its accompanying doctrines and thus adopt, practically speaking, a foreign, syncretistic form of Christianity. Over-contextualization is "high end syncretism" where there is a lack of engagement and knowledge of the Scriptures in the receiving culture. Thus culture overwhelms and dilutes the truth of the gospel and develops a "lazy tolerance" of old beliefs and practices. Healthy contextualization demands a proper "exegesis of Scriptures and culture." See Larry Owens, "Syncretism and the Scriptures," *Evangelical Missions Quarterly*, January 2007 (Volume 43, Number 1), pp. 74-80.

3. Dependency can be healthy or unhealthy. Healthy dependency is characterizd by interdependency within the Body of Christ. Since there is but one Body and all are members, all belong and all are needed for the Body to function properly (1 Corinthians 12). All members are needed to mutually support and complement one another. Unhealthy dependency can occur in missions when there is a continuing one-way flow of money or personnel. As with adult children, parents may initially help them "stand on their own two feet" financially, but eventually they are expected to earn their own way. So with a developing national church, the dependence on outside resources will reduce as it becomes more self-supporting and self-governing. See Daniel Rickett, *Building Strategic Relationships: a Practical Guide to Partnering with Non-Western Missions* (Partners International, 2000).

4. James the brother of Jesus was one of the leading elders in Jerusalem. He, along with the apostles, met with Paul and Barnabas to discuss the basis of the inclusion of Gentiles in the household of faith. Their conclusion that all, whether Jew or Gentile, are saved through grace, apart from circumcision and obedience to the Law of Moses, had far reaching implications for the spread of the gospel in the Gentile world (Acts 15:13-29).

5. No leader can fulfill his ministry alone. It takes a team. Doing church as a team requires a type of structure that can easily be duplicated, a "fractal pattern." An organic structure is one with living parts that move and

work together as a whole such as the human body. The Church as the Body of Christ is more like a living organism than a static organization. "Doing church as a team uses this same fractal design. It is a very simple, duplicable pattern that is found in most organisms. Each one has similar patterns and similar purposes." Building a team of four or five people with similar ministry passions (such as infants, children, youth, adults, people in need etc.) whose different giftings and abilities can work together to accomplish a common purpose is a "fractal pattern." It can readily be duplicated as the ministry grows with each member of the team developing a team of four or five people who eventually in turn will do the same. See Wayne Cordeiro, *Doing Church as a Team: Launching Effective Ministries Through Teamwork* (New Hope Publishers, 1998), pp. 185-206, and George Barna, *The Power of Team Leadership: Finding Strength in Shared Responsibility* (Waterbrook Press, 2001).

6. Five types of leaders have been identified each with increasing spheres of influence: type I – local volunteer lay leaders, direct face-to-face influence (small group leaders, Sunday school teachers, worship leaders, youth sponsors, prayer leaders, etc); type II – local volunteer leaders of lay leaders, direct face-to-face influence (Sunday school superintendent; elders, deacons etc.); type III – local paid bi-vocational or full-time leaders, direct and indirect community influence (pastors of smaller congregations); type IV – paid full-time leaders, direct and indirect regional influence (pastors and associate pastors of larger congregations; leaders of Christian ministries; circuit-riding pastors; divisional superintendents; district supervisors, etc.); type V – national and international leaders, largely indirect influence (presidents of national boards; global council leaders, itinerant apostolic, prophetic, evangelistic, teaching and pastoral leaders, etc). Each type requires a different kind of training. The greater the sphere of influence the greater the need for specialized training, especially types IV and V. See Edgar J. Elliston, *Home Grown Leaders* (Wm. Carey Library, 1992), pp. 26-35.

7. Planned spontaneity is the paradox of Spirit-bred and Spirit-led evangelism. Acts 1:8 seems to suggest both the spontaneous working of the Holy Spirit and planned progression of the expanding witness to Christ by his Spirit-empowered followers. The Apostle Paul's journeys also appear to include something of both spontaneous (Acts 16:6-10) and planned elements (Acts 15:36; 17:1, 2). One contemporary example of such planned spontaneity in evangelism is the "treasure hunt" where the Holy Spirit reveals "clues" concerning people ("lost coins or treasures") He wants found. Using the "clues" the evangelism team goes into the community looking for the individuals or groups whom the Lord has "highlighted" and prepared to receive the good news of a gospel of forgiveness, healing and deliverance. Such Book-of-Acts type encounters between

believers and seekers (like Philip and the Ethiopian eunuch, and Peter and Cornelius) are described in the book *The Ultimate Treasure Hunt: a Guide to Supernatural Evangelism through Supernatural Encounters* (Destiny Image Publishers, 2007) by Kevin Dedmon.

8. Cooperative evangelism is most fruitful when evangelistic events are connected with the planting of new churches for the new believers. See C. Peter Wagner, *Strategies for Church Growth: Tools for Effective Mission and Evangelism* (Regal Books, 1987), pp. 168-170.

9. Church planting movements where "a rapid and exponential increase of indigenous churches planting churches within a given people group or population segment" is a key in evangelizing a region (David Garrison, *Church Planting Movements*, Richmond, VA: International Mission Board of the Southern Baptist Convention, 1999, p. 7). From his research of church planting movements in Latin America, China, India and Cambodia, Garrison has identified ten common factors that have characterized every movement: 1) worship in the heart language of the people; 2) relational webs of evangelism; 3) rapid incorporation of new converts into the church; 4) passion and fearlessness in witness; 5) a high level of commitment to become a Christian; 6) societal crises create a ripe environment for the gospel; 7) on-the-job training for church leaders; 8) de-centralization of authority in leadership; 9) minimize foreignness with outsiders (missionaries) keeping a low profile; 10) missionaries willing to endure hardness as good soldiers of Jesus Christ. Also see Jim Montgomery, <u>New Testament Fire in the Philippines</u> (Manila, Philippines: C-GRIP, 1972) and *Dawn 2000: 7 Million Churches to Go* (Pasadena, CA: WM. Carey Library, 1989).

Chapter Six

1. "All the world in all the Word" reflects a major theme of Scripture. What is the Bible *all* about? Is it *all* about anything? What binds together the sixty-six books of the Bible written over a period of about 1500 years? It is about God's passion to redeem *all*. It is about the depth of his love in sending his Son, and the breadth of his love in that his death was for all humankind. See H. Cornell Goerner, *All Nations in God's Purpose: What the Bible Teaches about Missions* (Broadman Press, 1979).

2. John Piper writes: "God has given us prayer because Jesus has given us a mission…The missionary enterprise advances by prayer…(God's) missionary purpose (is) that the nations worship him. He will secure this triumph by entering into the warfare and becoming the main combatant. And he will make that engagement plain to all the participants *through prayer*. Because prayer shows that the power is from the Lord…consider

the amazing scope of prayer in the vibrant missionary life of the early church" (*Let the Nations Be Glad! The Supremacy of God in Missions*, Baker Books, 1993, pp. 47, 57).

3. It is estimated that approximately 3 percent of the world's population (200 million) have crossed international boundaries and currently live in a country other than that of their birth (Adam Roberts, "Special Report: Migration, Open Up", *Economist*, January 3, 2008). Millions more have moved within the country in which they were born, many to large urban areas seeking a better life. Such international immigration and national migration has resulted in demographic shifts in urban populations, requiring cross-cultural evangelism and church planting. Reaching such ethnically diverse populations calls for the church to think missiologically, to think "missions." The establishing of "ethnic congregations" including language specific congregations will need to be considered, especially churches in changing, transitional communities. See Jere Allen and George Bullard, *Shaping a Future for the Church in the Changing Community* (Home Missions Board Southern Baptist Convention, 1981) for ethnic ministry in churches in multi-cultural areas.

4. The decision of the Jerusalem Council concerning Gentiles had two dimensions: relationship to God and relationships within the Church. Clearly the conclusion of the Council was that both Jews and Gentiles are saved by grace through faith in Jesus Christ, for "whoever calls upon the name of the Lord shall be saved." Circumcision was not a pre-requisite for salvation for either Jew or Gentile. However, Jews were not encouraged to stop the practice of circumcising their children and no longer live according to their customs. The Apostle Paul was wrongly accused of so teaching Jews who lived among the Gentiles (Diaspora Jews). To show there was no truth to this accusation Paul was asked by the Jewish believers in Jerusalem to join in the purification rites of four Jewish believers who had made a vow and to pay their expenses so they could have their heads shaved. This Paul did to show that although observing of the Law was not necessary to be saved, living according to Jewish customs was proper and legitimate (Acts 21:20-25). In other words, Jews who believed in the Messiah could continue to live as Jews, They did not have to stop being Jewish to be Christians. A distinction was made between cultural practices and salvation. However, as such customs pertained to Gentiles the four prohibitions in the decision of the "Jerusalem Council" were all they were asked to observe because "Moses has been preached in every city from the earliest times and is read in the synagogues on every Sabbath" (Acts 15:20, 21). As members of the Body of Christ believing Gentiles were encouraged to "make every effort to keep the unity of the Spirit in the bond of peace" (Ephesians 4:3). Dwelling together in unity was essential because there is only "one body and one Spirit, one hope, one Lord, one faith, one

baptism and one God and Father of all, who is over all and through all and in all" (Ephesians 4:4-6).

5. God's eternal covenant with His people was threefold: a) He would be their God; b) They would be his people; c) He would dwell among them (see Exodus 29:45, 46; Deuteronomy 29: 12, 13; Jeremiah 31:33; Ezekiel 37:37, 38). This covenant finds its fulfillment in Jesus Christ, "the mediator of the new covenant" (Hebrews 8:10; 9:15) who through His sacrifice opened a new and living way to the Father, bringing lost people into relationship with God and into his family, and who through the gift of the Holy Spirit comes to dwell with and within his people (John 14:17, 18). This covenant will have its ultimate and climactic fulfillment in the New Jerusalem when "the dwelling of God is with men, and he will live with them and they will be his people (literally, "peoples"), and God himself will be with them and be their God" (Revelation 21:3). And this covenant includes "a great multitude...from every nation, tribe, people and language" (Revelation 7:9).

6. Evangelism has been categorized based on the spiritual and cultural "distance" between the believer and the unbeliever. E-0 (evangelism 0) is the process of leading persons to Christ who are already church attendees or members. E-1 (evangelism 1) involves leading people to Christ who are of the same culture as the believer. The "distance" is spiritual between those who are part of the Body of Christ, the Church, and those who are not. E-2 (evangelism 2) is cross-cultural evangelism. In addition to the spiritual "distance" is a cultural "distance" which involves reaching a person of a similar culture such as an English-speaking Anglo ministering to a Spanish-speaking Hispanic. E-3 (evangelism 3) is the same as E-2 but involves a greater "cultural distance" such as an English-speaking Anglo reaching a Mandarin-speaking Chinese person. See C. Peter Wagner, *Strategies for Church Growth: Tools for Effective Mission and Evangelism*, Ventura, CA: Regal Books, 1987, p. 116.

7. Don Richardson in his book *Eternity in Their Hearts: the Untold Story of Christianity among Folk Religions of Ancient People* (Regal Books, 1981) suggests that "the hidden message of Acts" is the reluctance of the 12 apostles to carry out Christ's Great Commission to "disciple the nations." He writes concerning the Jerusalem Council, "It is possible that some of the original apostles...finally began to open their eyes at this point to the possibilities of ministry among far-away Gentiles. Hearing Paul and Barnabas report large scale response among Asian peoples may have forced them to realize at last that Jerusalem and Samaria were not the only places "where the action was" (p. 168).

8. In 1982 a gathering of mission leaders sponsored by the Lausanne Strategy Working Group was called together to bring clarity and definition to the remaining missions task. Two basic definitions came from this

meeting: a) a "people group" is a significantly large grouping of individuals who perceive themselves to have a common affinity for one another because of their shared language, religion, ethnicity, occupation, class or caste situation. It is the largest group within which the gospel can spread as a church planting movement without encountering barriers of understanding or acceptance; b) an unreached people group is a group within which there is no indigenous community of believing Christians able to evangelize this people group. See Ralph D. Winter and Bruce A. Koch, "Finishing the Task: the Unreached Peoples Challenge" in *Perspectives on the World Christian Movement: a Reader*, Third Edition (William Carey Library, 1999), p. 514. Although these definitions are somewhat imprecise, "God probably did not intend for us to use a precise definition of people groups so as to think we could ever stop doing pioneer missionary work just because we conclude that all the groups within our definition have been reached…The point rather is that as long as the Lord has not returned, there must be more people groups to reach, and we should keep on reaching them" (John Piper, *Let the Nations Be Glad! The Supremacy of God in Missions*, p. 205).

9.   "One of the great untold stories of Christianity in this (the twentieth) century has been the astounding growth of vital, indigenous Christianity in nearly every country of the world" writes Patrick Johnstone in his book *The Church is Bigger Than You Think: the Unfinished Work of World Evangelism* (Christian Focus Publications, 1998), p. 109.

10. It was Luis Bush, the international director of the AD2000 & Beyond Movement, who coined the phrase "10/40 Window." The "Joshua Project 2000: helped focus outreach to the 1700+ least reached groups of 10,000 or more in population, most of which are in the "10/40 Window." With the planned closing of the AD2000 & Beyond Movement at the end of the year 2000, a new ongoing ministry by former AD2000 staff members has been formed called "Joshua Project II." It is an expansion of the original "Joshua Project 2000" which includes all the least reached peoples of the world irrespective of size. Information and updates can be obtained through the "Joshua Project II" email address (survey@joshuaproject.net) and website (http://www.joshuaproject.net).

Conclusion

1.   John Piper, *Let the Nations Be Glad!: the Supremacy of God in Missions* (Grand Rapids, MI: Baker, 1993), p. 35.

Bibliography

Allen, Jere and George Bullard, *Shaping a Future for the Church in the Changing Community*. Richmond, VA: Home Missions Board Southern Baptist Convention, 1981.

Allen, Roland, *Missionary Methods: St. Paul's or Ours.* Grand Rapids, MI: Wm. B. Eerdmans Publishing Co., 1967 reprint.

Amstutz, John L, "Beyond Pentecost: a Study of Some Sociological Dimensions of New Testament Church Growth from the Book of Acts," *Essays on Apostolic Themes.* Paul Elbert, Editor, Peabody, MA: Hendrikson Publishers, 1985, pages 208-225.

Amstutz, John L, "Foursquare Missions: Doing More with Less," *Pneuma* (Spring 1994), pages 63-80.

Balda, Wesley D., *Heirs of the Same Promise: Using Acts as a Study Guide for Evangelizing Ethnic America.* Monrovia, CA: MARC, 1984.

Barna, George, *The Power of Team Leadership: Finding Strength through Shared Responsibility.* Colorado Springs, CO: WaterBrook Press, 2001.

Barrett, David B, George T. Kurian and Todd M. Johnson, *World Christian Encyclopedia*, second edition, volume 1. New York, NY: Oxford University Press, 2001.

Brown, Daniel and Ralph Moore, editors, *Understanding the Times: Key Issues for the Local Church in the 21st Century.* Kaneohe, HI: Straight Street Publications, 1994.

Cordeiro, Wayne, *Doing Church as a Team: Launching Effective Ministries Through Teamwork*. Honolulu, HI: New Hope Publishers, 1998.

Dedmon, Kevin, *The Ultimate Treasure Hunt: a Guide to Supernatural Evangelism through Supernatual Encounters*. Shippensburg, PA: Destiny Image Publishers, 2007.

Dowley, Tim, editor, *Eerdmans' Handbook to the History of Christianity*. Grand Rapids, MI: Wm. B. Eerdmans Publishing Co., 1977.

Edwards, Leland, *Chasing the Vision*. Lake Mary, Fl: Creation House/Foursquare Media, 2006.

Garrison, David, *Church Planting Movements*. Richmond, VA: International Mission Board Southern Baptist Convention, 1999.

Getz, Gene, *Sharpening the Focus of the Church*. Chicago, IL: Moody Press, 1974.

Getz, Gene, *The Measure of a Man*. Ventura, CA: Regal Books, 1974.

Goerner, H. Cornell, *All Nations in God's Purpose: What the Bible Teaches About Missions*. Nashville, TN: Broadman Press, 1979.

Johnstone, Patrick, *The Church is Bigger than You Think: the Unfinished Work of World Evangelism*. Rossshire, Great Britain, Christian Focus Publications, 1998.

Keyes, Lawrence W., *The Last Age of Missions: a Study of Third World Mission Societies*. Pasadena, CA: Wm. Carey Library, 1983.

McClung, Grant, Jr., "Pentecostal/Charismatic Perspectives on a Missiology for the Twenty-first Century," *Pneuma* 16 (Spring 1994), pages 11-22.

McGavran, Donald, *The Bridges of God: a Study in the Strategy of Missions*. New York: Friendship Press, 1955.

McPherson, Aimee Semple, *This is That*. Los Angeles, CA; Bridal Call Publishing House, 1921.

Montgomery, Jim, *DAWN 2000: 7 Million Churches to Go*. Pasadena, CA: Wm. Carey Library, 1989.

Montgomery, Jim, *New Testament Fire in the Philippines*. Manila: C-GRIP, 1972.

Owens, Larry, "Syncretism and the Scriptures," *Evangelical Missions Quarterly* (January 2007), pages 74-80.

Pate, Larry D., *From Every People: a Handbook of Two-thirds World Missions*. Monrovia, CA: MARC, 1989.

Piper, John, *Let the Nations be Glad! The Supremacy of God in Missions*. Grand Rapids, Baker Books, 1993.

Piper, John, *What Jesus Demands from the World*. Wheaton, IL: Crossway Books, 2006.

Richardson, Alan, "Poor," *A Theological Word Book of the Bible*. New York, NY: McMillan Publishing Co., Inc., 1950.

Richardson, Don, *Eternity in Their Hearts: the Untold Story of Christianity among Folk Religions of Ancient People*. Ventura, CA: Regal Books, 1981.

Rickert, Daniel, *Building Strategic Relationships: a Practical Guide to Partnering with Non-Western Missions*. Brampton, Ontario, Canada: Partners International, 2000.

Schell, Steve, editor, *Women in Leadership Ministry*. Los Angeles, CA: Foursquare Media, 2007.

Sider, Ron, *Rich Christians in an Age of Hunger*. Downers Grove, IL: InterVarsity Press, 1977.

Van Engen, Charles, *God's Missionary People: Rethinking the Purpose of the Local Church*. Grand Rapids: Baker Book House, 1993.

Wagner, C. Peter, *Church Planting for a Great Harvest: a Comprehensive Guide*. Ventura, CA: Regal Books, 1990.

Wagner, C. Peter, *On the Crest of the Wave*. Ventura, CA: Regal Books, 1983.

Wagner, C. Peter, *Stop the World I Want to Get On*. Ventura, CA: Regal Books, 1973.

Wagner, C. Peter, *Strategies for Church Growth: Tools for Effective Mission and Evangelism*. Ventura, CA: Regal Books, 1987.

Wagner, C. Peter, *Your Spiritual Gifts Can Help Your Church Grow*. Ventura, CA: Regal Books, 1994

Winter, Ralph D. and Bruce A. Koch, "Finishing the Task: the Unreached Peoples Challenge," *Perspectives on the World Christian Movement: a Reader*. Ralph D. Winter and Steven C. Hawthorne, editors, Pasadena, CA: Wm. Carey Library, 1999, pages 509-524.

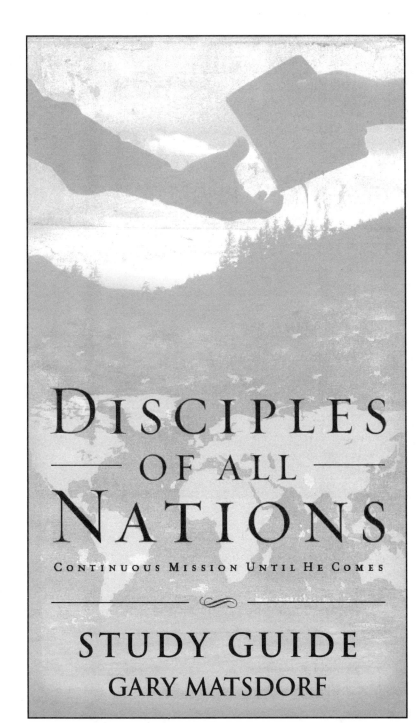

DISCIPLES
— OF ALL —
NATIONS

CONTINUOUS MISSION UNTIL HE COMES

STUDY GUIDE
GARY MATSDORF

Please note: All page numbers referenced in each of the "B" sections (Processing the Chapter) are incorrect. The number found at the end of each question is off by two (i.e. page 13 should read "page 11", page 14 should read "page 12", page 15 should read "page 13" etc.)

Disciples of All Nations:
Luke's Story

A. BIBLE READING
(to be done <u>before</u> reading the chapter)

1. According to Matthew 24:14, what is the scope of the Church's assignment with reference to the gospel message?

2. According to Romans 15:19, 23 how far had the gospel spread by the time of this writing?

3. According to Colossians 1:6, how effective did Paul perceive the gospel to be by that time in history?

4. Read Acts 2:42-47. What impact did the wonders and signs performed by the apostles have on the people? What was the result?

5. According to Acts 11:18, what was the assessment of many Jews in response to Peter's report about earlier events at Cornelius' house?

6. According to Acts 15:11, what must the Church always remember as it fulfills its global assignment of making disciples?

B. PROCESSING THE CHAPTER
(to be completed after reading)

1. What did Jesus expect of the original Eleven and how did they respond to His expectation (page 13)?

2. Within less than 30 years, how far geographically had the Church gotten with Jesus' original assignment (page 13)?

3. Reading Acts carefully, where did the early Church "plant" strategic churches that then penetrated surrounding areas with the gospel (page 14)?

4. What prompted the spread of the gospel to Samaria and beyond (page 16)?

5. What is the significance of the men mentioned in Acts 13:1 who joined Paul and Barnabas as leaders in the church at Antioch in Syria (page 17)?

6. What was different about Paul and Barnabas' missionary work launched from Antioch as compared to that initially launched into Samaria (page 17)? Among whom was their work?

7. What are some implications of the decision by the Jerusalem Council in terms of world-wide evangelism today (page 18)?

8. What is the significance of Paul's "Macedonian vision" in terms of fulfilling Acts 1:8 (page 18)?

9. What do you see as some important implications in terms of evangelizing nations of Paul not only planting churches but staying in Ephesus for two years to teach the converts (pages 18-19)?

10. In addition to the apostles, who helped carry out Jesus' commission to "make disciples of all nations" (page 19)?

11. What four stages of National Church Development can be learned from carefully following Luke's story in Acts (page 20)? What is significant about this four-stage pattern for us today (page 22)?

C. MAKING APPLICATION—

1. What was biblically new or challenging to you in this chapter and why?

2. Luke emphasizes repeatedly the importance of Holy Spirit fullness in "making disciples." What does being Spirit-filled mean to you personally and how do you maintain Spirit fullness in your life?

3. The observation is made that "the 'making of disciples of all nations' was carried out by a Spirit-filled and Spirit-directed church who, with the apostles, were witnesses to the ends of the earth." Can you see yourself "making disciples of all nations"? Why or why not? If yes...how specifically do you envision yourself doing that?

4. What practical challenge sparked in your heart while reading this chapter? What would be your next step in responding to that challenge?

5. Which of the four stages do you see yourself as best gifted, equipped and called to do? Do you see yourself involved in that phase of ministry outside your nation?

6. If you are a Lead Pastor/National Leader of a church/nation who will not leave your country but want to participate in "making disciples of all nations," do you see any missiological adjustments your church/nation could make in response to this chapter?

7. If you are preparing to deploy to another country, what do you want to make sure you remember and apply from this chapter?

CHAPTER ONE

Disciples of All Nations:
Foursquare's Story

A. BIBLE READING
(to be done <u>before</u> reading the chapter)

1. What does Hebrews 13:8 say about Jesus and what does this imply about His promise to baptize people with the Holy Spirit today?

2. According to 1 Timothy 2:4-6, what is God's will that every Christian must clearly remember and emphasize as part of their life?

3. According to 1 Corinthians 12:7-11, what are the Holy Spirit's manifestations available to all Christ followers today to enhance ministry to hurting people?

B. PROCESSING THE CHAPTER
(to be completed after reading)

1. What is inscribed on the cornerstone of Angelus Temple in Los Angeles and what does this inscription express about Foursquare since its inception (page 23)?

2. What did Sister McPherson believe about the availability in her generation, and ours, of the Spirit's power as demonstrated at Pentecost (page 23)?

3. Who was the primary audience of early 20th century missionaries and how did Arthur Edwards change this common strategy when pioneering Panama for Foursquare (page 24)?

4. What was distinct about Foursquare Panama by 1940 (page 24)?

5. What was the second country evangelized by Foursquare in Latin America and what was the primary strategy for evangelizing (page 25)?

6. When and where did Foursquare make substantial progress in establishing ministry in Africa (page 26)?

7. What is meant in saying, "'Home missions' was happening in Nigeria," and what happened to the role of the American missionaries as the Foursquare ministry expanded in Nigeria (pages 26-27)?

8. What common strategy characterizes Foursquare Latin America and Foursquare Africa (page 27)?

9. In what country did Foursquare Asia begin and what was an important factor in establishing Foursquare in this country (pages 27-28)?

10. Has Foursquare Philippines become a "sending nation"? If so, where have its missionaries gone (pages 28-29)?

11. What spiritual elements face Foursquare ministry in countries like New Guinea, Sri Lanka and Cambodia (page 29)?

12. On what continent did Foursquare not make much progress until the 1980s and why (page 29)?

13. At the time of the writing of this book, in how many countries did Foursquare have a ministry presence and what was the annual percent of growth (page 30)?

14. What three elements has "God consistently blessed" as the Foursquare gospel has expanded around the world and why (pages 30-31)?

C. MAKING APPLICATION—

1. How, specifically, do you practice God's will in 1 Timothy 2:4-6 in your life on a regular basis?

2. What has been your experience in terms of being used by the Holy Spirit in any of the 1 Corinthians 12 manifestations of the Spirit, such as healing? Do you see these displays of the Spirit's power as integral to your ministry, like it was in that of many early Foursquare missionaries? Why...or why not?

3. Which region(s) of the world addressed in this chapter (other than your own) do you have the greatest personal passion for and why? If you are a Lead Pastor/National Leader of a church/nation, how are you implementing your passion in your church/nation to partner with FMI (or the missions department of your nation) in ministry in that region?

4. What spoke to you personally the most in this chapter?

Disciples of All Nations:
National Church Development

A. BIBLE READING
(to be done <u>before</u> reading the chapter)

1. What are we told to do in Mark 16:15?

2. According to Mark 16:17, what can we expect to accompany our proclamation of the gospel?

3. According to Matthew 28:19, what is a crucial "first step" in our evangelizing the lost?

4. According to Matthew 28:20, what are we to begin doing immediately following someone's salvation/water baptism experience?

5. Read Acts 1:8, write it out and begin to commit it to memory.

6. According to Acts 14:21-22, what did Paul and Barnabas see as necessary to do having initially planted churches in Lystra, Iconium and Antioch?

7. According to Acts 14:23, what else did they do in their church plants?

B. PROCESSING THE CHAPTER

(to be completed after reading)

1. In your own words, what is the PURPOSE of the Foursquare Church in every nation (page 34)?

2. In your own words, what is the MISSION of the Foursquare Church in every nation (page 34)?

3. In your own words, what is the STRATEGY of the Foursquare Church in every nation (page 34)?

4. Foursquare Missions' development is based on a four-stage model. What are the two steps ("from...to") of each stage (page 34)?

   • Stage 1:

   • Stage 2:

   • Stage 3:

   • Stage 4:

5. What is the goal of Stage 1 (pages 36-37)?

6. What is the goal of Stage 2 (page 38)?

7. What is the goal of Stage 3 (page 39)?

8. What is the goal of Stage 4 (page 40)?

9. Fill in the appropriate blank for each of these (pages 36-41).
   - Stage 1: INITIATE involves a two-fold process:
     _____ and _____.
   - Stage 2: NURTURE involves a two-fold process:
     _____ and _____.
   - Stage 3: EXPAND involves a two-fold process:
     _____ and _____.
   - Stage 4: SEND involves a two-fold process:
     _____ and _____.

10. What is the two-fold task of Stage 1 and what must be avoided (page 37)?

11. What is the two-fold task of Stage 2 and what must we avoid (pages 38-39)?

12. What is the two-fold task of Stage 3 and what must we be careful not to do relative to moving to Stage 3 (pages 39-40)?

13. What is the two-fold task of Stage 4 and what must we be careful not to do relative to moving to Stage 4 (pages 40-41)?

14. Stage 4 churches can be described as "_____ churches" (page 42).

C. MAKING APPLICATION—

1. If you are a National Leader of a nation, at what stage do you see your nation? If it is not yet a Stage 4 nation, do you have a strategic plan for taking the nation to the next Stage? If it is a Stage 4 nation, do you have a strategic plan for furthering its ministry? Please explain.

2. If you are preparing to deploy to another country, at what Stage is that country? If it is not yet a Stage 4 country, how do you see yourself partnering with the country's leadership to help get it to the next Stage? If it is a Stage 4 country, what do you perceive your specific role to be in the ongoing ministry development of the country?

3. If you are a Lead Pastor with a passion for a specific foreign field, do you know that field's Stage and how do you plan to specifically partner with the country's leadership to help it to the next Stage or to further develop a Stage 4 ministry?

4. Being totally honest with yourself and with others, which of these four Stages interests you most and which Stage is quite frankly a personal challenge to you...and why?

Chapter Three

Disciples of All Nations:
Stage One: Initiate—Evangelize

A. BIBLE READING
*(to be done **before** reading the chapter)*

1. Read Luke 4:16-21 and answer the following—

   • For what specifically was Jesus anointed with the Holy Spirit (vs. 18a)?

   • How does Jesus further describe His ministry (vv. 18b-19)?

2. According to Acts 10:38, what two things did Jesus do as a result of being "anointed with the Holy Spirit and power"?

3. According to Matthew 10:7-8, what assignment did Jesus give the Twelve that we are to carry on just as they did?

4. According to Romans 15:18-19, what two means did Paul use to evangelize?

5. According to John 3:36, what must we always keep clearly in focus in terms of people's eternal destiny?

6. According to Romans 10:14-15, what does Paul want us to remember in terms of people hearing the gospel message?

7. According to Matthew 4:19, what promise does Jesus make to us as His disciples?

8. According to 2 Peter 3:9, what is the core of God's heart relative to lost people?

9. What is Jesus' command to us in Matthew 5:16?

B. PROCESSING THE CHAPTER
(to be completed after reading)

1. What is the goal of Stage 1 and what is our two-fold task in this Stage (page 43)?

2. What two ways did Jesus and the Twelve use to communicate the gospel and what does the Book of Acts record relative to these means of evangelizing (page 44)?

3. Reflecting off Jesus' three parables in Luke 15, what three truths about lost people are we to remember as impetus to evangelize (pages 44-47)?

4. Refering to our call to evangelism, two tasks are before us concerning to the lost. What are they (page 46)?

5. What is meant by "primary fishing ponds" (page 47)?

6. What must accompany preaching of the basic gospel message and why (page 48)? What are some specifics given relative to this accompanying task?

7. What must we remember about evangelism...especially in under-evangelized, post-Christian or Muslim nations...lest we become overly anxious and susceptible to discouragement (pages 48-49)?

8. What is meant by "the bonding process" and what are its two-fold aspects (page 51)?

9. Once a person is "born again," we must help them to be immediately baptized in water, to receive the fullness of the Holy Spirit and to become an active part of what (page 52)?

10. Biblical discipleship is always within the context of what (page 52)? Also, what are we doing when we disciple someone (page 54)?

C. MAKING APPLICATION—

1. In assessing your life personally, about what percentage of your friends are unbelievers? Do you have meaningful contact with non-Christians, so as to be an influence for Christ in their lives? If not, why not...and do you see a need for change?

2. If you are a Lead Pastor, how does your church "do evangelism" so that your church growth has a healthy percentage of "kingdom growth" vs. "transfer growth"?

3. If you are a National Leader, how would you assess your country's overall evangelistic efforts? How, specifically, do you equip your leaders (especially the Lead Pastors) to effectively and regularly do the work of an evangelist?

4. How does the church of which you're a part identify new converts and begin the discipleship process? How would you assess your effectiveness in getting new converts from the point of "raising their hand to receive Jesus" to being baptized in water, filled with the Spirit, integrated into the life of the church and on the pathway to discipleship?

5. A bold statement is made in saying that "accompanying evangelism must be good deeds...the love of God in Christ is not only expressed in word, but in deed—practical deeds of kindness and acts of compassion." This is hotly debated in evangelicalism, even within Foursquare; most evangelicals espouse that there are many social and/or government agencies who "do acts of compassion" and that the Church's responsibility is preaching the Good News (known technically as "proclamation evangelism"). Do you agree that acts of kindness and of compassion (known technically as "presence or social service evangelism") are integral to effective evangelism and should be part of Stage 1 ministry? Why or why not?

CHAPTER FOUR

Disciples of All Nations:
Stage Two: Nurture—Strengthen

A. BIBLE READING
*(to be done **before** reading the chapter)*

1. What is the goal of discipleship as expressed in Colossians 1:28?

2. How does Paul define this same goal in Romans 8:29?

3. What analogy is used in Hosea 2:16 to describe God's relationship to His people?

4. What analogy does Paul use in Ephesians 5:31-32 to describe Christ's relationship to His followers?

5. According to Acts 2:46, where is one place the early Church met? Why did they meet there?

6. According to Acts 11:27-30, what is one way the early disciples showed their willingness to "help others like a family helps its own"?

7. According to Ephesians 5:2, what is one way we show we're mature disciples?

8. According to Ephesians 4:11-13, what is the main function of church leadership and for how long is this God's plan for leadership?

9. According to Titus 1:6, what are three key qualifications Paul looked for in church leaders?

10. According to Luke 22:27, what was the nature of Jesus' leadership that He intended to be reproduced in His followers (see also Mark 10:44)?

11. According to 1 Timothy 4:16, what two things must leaders watch closely as they disciple others?

B. PROCESSING THE CHAPTER

(to be completed after reading)

1. What is the goal of Stage 2 ministry and what is its twofold task (page 57)?

2. In what two primary arenas are we called to reflect Christ-like love and holiness (page 57)?

3. Who are the "primary disciplers" who lead Christ-followers in these two arenas and what two tasks are vital for effective discipling (pages 57-58)?

4. What was God's first "created institution" and for what is it His primary laboratory (page 58)?

5. Rather than provoking their children, what is the responsibility given parents in terms of bringing their children to maturity of faith (page 59)?

6. Complete this sentence: "The church is, in a sense, an _____(page 59)?

7. Complete this sentence: although the early Church was not communal, it "functioned as a _____" and as "an _____ family" (page 60).

8. What does the chapter teach was Christ's last request to His Father (page 61)?

9. In mentoring disciples, what must we help them develop and release as part of our Stage 2 ministry efforts (page 63)?

10. Note the primary equipping or preparing responsibility of each of the five-fold gifts in Ephesians 4:11 (pages 63-64)—

   • **Apostles** are ambassadors called and sent of God to:

   • **Prophets** are messengers of God called and anointed to:

   • **Evangelists** proclaim good news and are called and gifted to:

   • **Pastors** are shepherds called and set apart by God to:

   • **Teachers** are interpreters of God's Word called and appointed to:

11. The Church's five-fold equipping or preparing ministries are called to prepare disciples in _____ and _____, "both by _____ and _____" (page 64).

12. What is meant by "synergy of the Spirit" (page 64)?

13. Although skill/ministry ability is important for a leader, what areas of a leader's life are most important according to the qualifications listed in 1 Timothy and Titus (page 65)?

14. Jesus avidly disavowed jealousy among the Twelve, and repeatedly reminded them of the quality of servant leadership. How did He model servant leadership and what did He say characterizes such leadership (page 65)?

15. Complete this sentence: "Such _____ of leaders…is essential to the growth and expansion of the Church." How did Paul instruct Timothy to go about this multiplication (page 66)?

C. MAKING APPLICATION—

1. If you are part of a Stage 2 or higher nation, or are being deployed to or wanting to assist a Stage 2 or higher nation, how do you see yourself specifically helping to make responsible, reproducing leaders?

2. In assessing your congregation as a Lead Pastor or your nation as a National Leader, would you say it reflects healthy community and family dynamics…or truth be told, does it reflect more the qualities of an institutional "gathering place" to worship and be taught? If the latter, what personal or theological challenges has this chapter presented you and do you intend to make any changes?

3. What is your greatest personal challenge in being a "servant leader"?

4. Do you believe God has gifted and called you to one of the five-fold Ephesians 4:11 ministries? If so and you are preparing to deploy to a nation, is your assignment in keeping with the primary purpose of that ministry as defined here?

5. In assessing your life using the leadership qualities found in 1 Timothy and Titus, where do you see the Spirit having brought reasonable maturity? What traits "need the most attention" and how do you envision yourself growing in those areas?

6. What do you see as some of the greatest challenges in Christian families assuming the responsibilities and privileges addressed here in order to be healthy, strengthened families?

7. What do you see as some of the greatest challenges in your church/nation in mobilizing members to do the work of ministry or in cultivating biblical community?

CHAPTER FIVE

Disciples of All Nations:
Stage Three: Expand—Multiply

A. BIBLE READING
(to be done <u>before</u> reading the chapter)

1. According to Jude 3, what is our charge concerning "the faith that was once for all entrusted to the saints"?

2. What is the charge of 1 Peter 5:12 concerning "the true grace of God"?

3. According to 1 Timothy 5:17-18, what is one responsibility to which the local church is to aspire with reference to its primary leaders?

4. Read Acts 6:1-16. What was the problem they encountered? Who identified the problem and what was their solution?

5. Read Exodus 18:18-26. What was the problem Moses encountered? Who identified its solution and what was the solution?

6. What was Titus' pastoral charge in Titus 1:5?

7. According to Philippians 1:27, what attitudes did Paul encourage among the Philippians so the Gospel would expand in their community?

8. According to Acts 8:1-14, what was one element that contributed to the gospel multiplying throughout Palestine?

9. According to Matthew 24:14, what is the Church's highest priority—in good times or difficult times?

B. PROCESSING THE CHAPTER
(to be completed after reading)

1. What is the goal of Stage 3 ministry and what is its twofold task (page 69)?

2. In what two ways must a local church be empowered to develop without continual dependence on outside help (page 69)?

3. Fill in the blanks from the Chapter. "If a church is to be fruitful and multiple…it has to be released to develop in a way that is culturally _____ so that it can become truly _____" (page 70).

4. What must a local church do within its culture, even as the early leaders in Rome did, in order to effectively express the true grace of God (page 71)?

5. Complete this sentence from the Chapter: "The seed of the gospel is the same...but the _____ varies" (page 71).

6. What is the "principle of incarnation" and how does it affect a church expressing its common faith, loving unity and sound doctrine (page 72)?

7. What four elements are necessary to successfully contextualize a church within its culture (pages 72-73)?

8. What two components are vital in facilitating growth and ministry in a church or nation and what are some strategic questions to ask in assessing if these components are in operation (page 73)?

9. What does the overview of Acts (pages 73-74) reveal about church structure? What does this necessitate on the part of church and National Leaders (pages 75-76)?

10. Although a given church must reach its own "Jerusalem," what becomes necessary for a truly expanding witness within a region or nation (pages 76-77)?

11. According to the Chapter, in order for a church to most effectively enlarge its vision and sphere of influence, its leaders and members must "experience the Father's _____ ...learning to _____ what God _____ and _____ what God _____" (page 78).

12. Effective Stage 3 ministry requires not only that a congregation grow larger, but that it do what (page 78)?

13. Complete this sentence from the Chapter: "In Stage 3, the planting of new churches through shared resources becomes a _____" (page 82).

C. MAKING APPLICATION—

1. Contextualizing the Gospel, though biblical and necessary, is oftentimes more of an art than a science. From your own experience, what are some difficulties you've encountered in contextualizing the Gospel (including contemporizing how it's ministered)?

2. If you're a Lead Pastor or National Leader, would you say you're flexible and willing to restructure your church/national system to best meet unfolding needs…or truth be told, is such restructuring difficult for you? If the latter, why?

3. If you are an "emerging leader," what is your assessment of "older leaders'" willingness to help you discover, develop and deploy your spiritual gifting? Do you perceive them as "threatened" or "stuck" and how would you respond to a leader you perceived as "threatened or stuck" if encountered in your foreign assignment?

4. If you are a Lead Pastor or National Leader, what are you doing to enlarge your church/nation's vision to see lost people through God's eyes, people who are "sheep without a shepherd"?

5. How would you personally assess your commitment to church multiplication? If you are a Lead Pastor or National Leader, are you multiplying new congregations? If not, why? If so, what are 2-3 key things you've learned about church multiplication that you'd share with someone doing it for the first time?

6. How would you assess your personal awareness of the foreign culture in which you minister or are preparing to minister and what are you doing to develop a sensitivity to resist the temptation to "import your culture into that culture"?

CHAPTER SIX

Disciples of All Nations:
Stage Four: Send—Extend

A. BIBLE READING
(to be done <u>before</u> reading the chapter)

1. According to Genesis 12:3, to whom does God intend His messengers proclaim His message? How does Paul use this text in Galatians 3:8?

2. According to Luke 24:47, Jesus commissions us to take the gospel where?

3. According to Luke 24:45, what must God's Spirit do in our lives if we are going to grasp Jesus' commission to us?

4. According to Luke 24:49, Jesus commanded the Eleven and those with them to do what?

5. How did John identify Jesus in John 1:29?

6. According to Luke 11:1, what did the Twelve clearly ask of Jesus?

7. According to Matthew 9:38, what must we do in order to see the Great Commission effectively carried out?

8. According to Acts 13:1-3, what was the church at Antioch doing when God gave a clear word to send Saul and Barnabas out to minister?

9. What are we taught to pray in 1 Timothy 2:1-3?

B. PROCESSING THE CHAPTER

(to be completed after reading)

1. What is the stated goal of Stage 4 ministry and what is its twofold task (page 83)?

2. Fill in the blanks—Stage 4 countries both send and support both _____ and _____ missionaries (page 83).

3. Why was the early Church's ministry to the Samaritans considered "cross-cultural evangelism" or what we popularly call "missions," and what did it require that is still required of us today (page 84)?

4. How did the Hellenistic Jewish believers in the early Jerusalem Church respond to the persecution that scattered many of them into non-Jewish territory (page 85)?

5. Fill in the blanks—with Cornelius' conversion, within Israel non-jewish_____ were coming to Christ. _____ was happening (page 86).

6. What is absolutely necessary for God's heart for the world—the impetus of Stage 4 ministry—to be awakened within a congregation or nation? What helps increase such an awareness (pages 86-87)?

7. Though being persecuted, what constituted the core of the Jerusalem Church's prayers in Acts 4 (page 87)?

8. What must we "first see" if we're going to eventually develop into a "missions" person and what two barriers are likely to challenge our becoming such a person (pages 88-90)?

9. Who are often the "ripest field for harvest" within the large cities of most nations (page 90)?

10. What is required to effectively reach diverse cultural groups locally and within one's nation (page 91)?

11. What is required to effectively fulfill the Church's global mandate (page 91)?

12. What is essential in order for another "life cycle" to begin (a Stage 4 church/nation planting a Stage 1 work) (pages 93-94)?

13. What was Paul's "constant passion" that must also be ours for Stage 4 churches/nations to be equally impassioned to reproduce and start new Stage 1 works (page 94)?

14. Fill in the blank—as the Gospel spreads, it spreads not only geographically but _____. What are some insights we can learn from Acts about doing this well (page 96)?

15. In all our strategy and efforts, what must Stage 4 churches/nations keep as "the highest priority" in their Gospel expansion efforts among different peoples and nations (page 99)?

C. MAKING APPLICATION—

1. All of us have prejudices. What people group—ethnic, religious or life-style—represents your greatest personal challenge to love and see won to Christ? Why?

2. If you are a Lead Pastor/National Leader, how would you assess the effectiveness of your church/nation in doing the twofold Stage 4 task of "networking and partnering"? If either is weak, do you know why and do you have a strategic plan to strengthen what's weak?

3. How would you access your personal prayer life in terms of praying for the nations, for the global expansion of the Gospel? If it's not what you'd like it to be, have you thought of a plan for growth?

4. How open minded would you assess believers around you to be with reference to the Church's privilege of spreading the Gospel globally? As a "missions minded person," if you perceive them to be less open minded that you'd like, what are two or three ways you can practically challenge/help them to broaden their mindset?

5. If you are a Lead Pastor/National Leader of a Stage 4 church/nation with experience planting a new cross-cultural Stage 1 work, share a bit of the process involved in the plant; what you learned; what you'd do differently; some successes and some setbacks. (If you're not a Lead Pastor/National Leader but you have experience in this area, either as a participant in a plant or a former leader of a plant, feel free to share as well.)

6. In assessing your spiritual gifting, experience, passion and temperament, what do you see as your greatest strengths and weaknesses in terms of being involved in a Stage 1 cross-cultural plant by a Stage 4 church/nation?